MW00609153

HOW TO COACH
FOOTBALL'S RUNNING
TRAP GAME

How to Coach
Football's Running
Trap Game

Jerry H. Laycock

PARKER PUBLISHING COMPANY, INC.

West Nyack, N.Y.

To my parents,
whose encouragement and understanding
made my career in athletics possible,

and to my amiable wife
whose cooperation makes coaching
a more winsome profession.

© 1972 *by*

Parker Publishing Company, Inc.

West Nyack, N.Y.

*All rights reserved. No part of this
book may be reproduced in any form or
by any means, without permission in
writing from the publisher.*

Library of Congress Cataloging in Publication Data

Laycock, Jerry H   1934-
    How to coach football's running trap game.

    1. Football--Offense. I. Title.
GV951.8.L3   796.33'22   72-2887
ISBN 0-13-403766-9

Printed in the United States of America

How the trap
will help you

The trap is a devastating weapon which can be mastered by any high school offensive unit if the proper fundamentals are instilled in the team.

This premise is based on the supposition that the coaching staff has a thorough knowledge of the fundamentals, a practice program incorporating good teaching procedures, and is using a well tested trap play formula. This book is designed to supply the high school coach with these elements.

The two simple trap formulas discussed in this book may be run from any offensive series.

This book does not cover another complete system of offense different from yours. It discusses trap plays only. It is written to assist high school coaches in perfecting trap plays in their offense. The successful trap rules and the technical points in teaching them are covered. Counter traps, flow traps, reverse traps, and draw traps are diagrammed and dissected.

To successfully execute any plays, the coach must understand the offense, know what the players are required to do and teach the techniques well. The trap play is no exception. However, after

9

reviewing this material the coach will find it is no more difficult to perform the trap well than any other play.

Certainly there are many ways to beat any particular defense, but every method relies on proper execution. Using the trap as a basic play will add new dimensions to the offense. The trap places great pressure on a number of aspects in the opponent's defensive plan that he does not otherwise have to consider.

Today most high school defensive units can force a back to string out the wide play, jam power plays and rush passers with ferocious intensity. Effective use of the trap will cut down greatly on the pursuit of the wide play and often slow the pass rush to a cautious hit and flow pattern. The threat of the trap can also force an opponent into many hours of contemplation before pre-rotating defenses to combat offensive power sets. These things can be accomplished by teaching a trap formula which can be mastered by any high school line through proper drills and dedicated practice time.

To implement the trap effectively in a particular established offense, a few techniques may need to be altered. With this in mind a description of fundamentals is the first area of discussion.

It is hoped that this presentation of fundamentals, practice programs, drills, and trap knowledge will be of aid in helping your team run more effective trap plays.

—Jerry Laycock

Contents

1

Coaching Team Fundamentals and Blocking Principles for the Running Trap Game

The importance of running the trap well in any offense can be readily seen as we quickly examine great trap plays of the past and see how outstanding teams have employed them.

As with the offenses of previous decades, our fundamentals in the line and backfield were arrived at through many years of experimentation. We feel, however, that our unique combination of fundamentals and procedures enable us to execute a multiple offense with a high degree of perfection. We have also found that the blocking principles are simple enough to be mastered by players of average ability, yet the rules have a flexibility which aids us in making simple adjustments quickly.

The split line play, quarterback pivots, backfield running lanes and blocking techniques all combine to complement our trapping game from any formation or play series we desire to use.

1

TRADITION OF THE TRAPPING GAME

The trap has played an important role in the history of football. Even though formations, techniques, equipment and rules have changed drastically since the 1930's, some factors have remained constant. One of these consistencies is that all of the great teams have relied on the trap to furnish the long gainer through the interior of the defensive line. Certainly the trap ranks with the sweep, pass, and belly options as a major offensive weapon. In tracing the development of the game, we find that every new formation and alignment has preserved the trap as an integral part of its offense.

From the thirties to the mid-forties the Notre Dame box and single wing dominated the scene. Teams crunched their way through game after game with power plays combined with a wide sweep. Because the fullback received the ball and did most of the faking by spinning, the quarterback was used as a blocker. This meant the offense could trap with pulling linemen or with the quarterback who was close to the line in an ideal trapping position.

As the teams developed this potential for the trap, it became a major instrument of destruction that enabled smaller teams to equalize the devastating power of awesome defensive units. One example from this era can be found in the ever exciting series be-

tween the University of Michigan and Michigan State. Before their
1934 meeting the University of Michigan had beaten Michigan State
for nineteen straight years. In fact the University hadn't lost a game
since 1931. State was much the smaller team that year. Their game
plan was to rely on trap plays to penetrate the gigantic Michigan
line. After using the standard off tackle plays from the Notre Dame
box formation, the fullback started keeping the ball up the middle
on the short trap. The trapper was the quarterback, one of the
smallest men on either squad.

Diagram 1: Fullback spinner trap from Notre Dame box

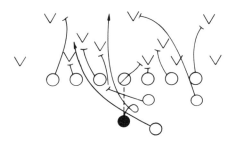

As soon as the guard became inside conscious, State blocked
him in and trapped the tackle out using two blockers, a guard and
quarterback.

Diagram 2: Halfback off tackle trap from Notre Dame box

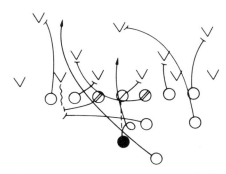

State used this combination of traps to defeat Michigan sixteen
to zero that day in one of the greatest games of their series.

With the advent of the "Tight T" in the mid-forties, the trap
was limited to using pulling linemen as the trapper because the
backs all became involved in running and faking patterns. The tight

line was conducive to power blocking with two-times and traps, however. The unbalanced line still remained in the limelight. This alignment enabled the teams to continue their use of the power play to the strong side. They still used the trap to split the tight interior defensive sets.

Diagram 3: Trap right from unbalanced "Tight T"

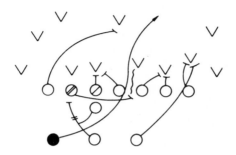

The defenses were fairly standard for most teams and the trap worked well in combating these sets because there was often a two-time block on each side of the hole.

The straight fullback trap from a balanced line, "T" set, was popularized by Notre Dame during this period. The center and trapping guard cross blocked while the tackles cut off the linebackers. The fullback went straight ahead at the snap of the ball.

Diagram 4: Notre Dame fullback trap

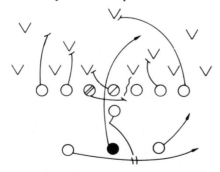

This has been one of the most copied plays in football.

Another unique play developed during this period was the Angsman trap in which the tackle did the pulling. From the "T" set the quarterback usually faked to the fullback and handed back to a halfback.

Diagram 5: Angsman style trap

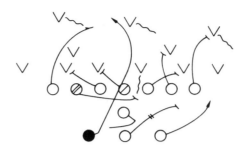

Modern versions of this trap have destroyed many defensive keys.

In the late forties many teams also experimented with the double wing. Wingback sets made it possible to trap with a back from the outside, in. One such trap was the tailback outside-in trap.

Diagram 6: Double wing outside-in trap

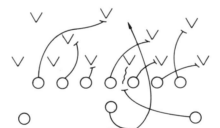

In the early fifties the "split T" caught on. Bud Wilkinson developed the split line concept at Oklahoma after working with Don Faurot, the Missouri coach. The "split T" was designed to hit over a wide area for short gains with quickness and thereby maintain possession of the ball longer. The system minimized the teaching of complicated techniques and plays because most of the blocking was one-on-one. However, rotating defenses and quicker interior pursuit soon caught up with the "split T" option as a sole means of attack and the trap became more and more prominent in combination with the split line. The fullback counter was one of the first "split T" plays to be combined with trap blocking.

It was soon found that the trap provided the long gainer on the ground needed in the "split T" offense. With the addition of re-

Diagram 7: "Split T" fullback counter

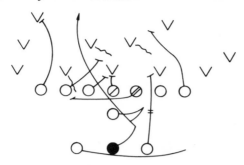

verses that required the pulling guards to block out on the ends, the pulling and trapping game was again firmly entrenched as a major part of every modern offense.

The sixties brought to offensive football extreme complications. Coaches learned to combine the split and power "T" with pro sets. The "I" formation brought single wing concepts back into focus. Teams began to run for daylight against complex defensive keys and sets. In general the offense changed to deeper handoffs, more counters, reverses, delay plays and again the trap emerged as a basic interior blocking formula taught by most coaches.

The "I" made great use of the traps that were previously run from the "T," such as the quick hitting fullback trap, plus it added slower developing trap plays like the tailback trap. This play is often run up the center with the tackle doing the trapping.

Diagram 8: Tailback trap—tackle pulling

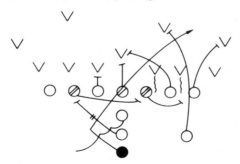

Green Bay perfected the power sweep from the pro set formation and used the off tackle trap to hold the interior pursuit to a minimum. Stanford then had great success with the same series at the college level.

Diagram 9: Green Bay series off tackle trap

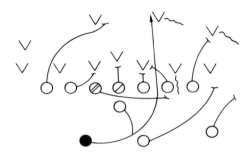

The pro set offenses were given a new look in the late sixties with the addition of the Houston triple option. A major counter used by triple option teams is the quick trap.

Diagram 10: Pro set—triple option fake—quick trap

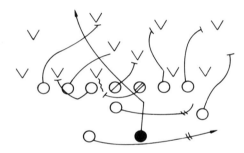

Reviewing some of the great trap plays used over the past few decades helps us to realize the excitement traps add to any offense at any level of play. Most coaches understand the need for such plays, but feel that they do not have the practice time needed to develop traps. Certainly there has long been a need for blocking rules and techniques that would enable a high school team to use a multiple offense and a variety of approaches to blocking. The problem has been to simplify trap blocking to a point that high school teams can perfect trap plays in the short time that they have to devote to them. We feel we have accomplished this step.

We are so confident of our players' ability to learn to block any defensive set with our trap formula and blocking techniques that our offense is based on the trap. The tighter the situation or more complicated the defense, the more we turn to a trap call.

In our final game of the 1969 season we faced an undefeated opponent who lead the conference in allowing the least yardage gained. In the opening minutes of play we drove down inside their ten yard line. After a penalty and a couple of short gains, we were faced with a fourth and seven situation against a strong goal line defense. Most teams expect the pass at this point. However, we were sure of a hard interior rush and we knew our best chance for the long gain was a trap. Because we had worked on this phase of our game, we were able to make the call we desired. We came out in a slot set to spread the defense and force them to cover wide. The quarterback faked a sprintout pass handing the ball to the right half on a draw trap. He ambled into the end zone untouched. We went on to win the game twenty to fourteen by using the draw trap in two more critical situations from different sets.

We feel that part of this success lies in our selection of basic fundamentals. The following techniques have assisted us in developing not only an expert trapping game, but also a sound total offense.

2

SIMPLIFIED LINE BLOCKING TECHNIQUES

Our offense requires linemen to move in a variety of directions. They must execute not only straight ahead blocks, but cross blocks, post and power blocks, and pull on traps and sweeps. A well balanced four point stance has proven to be surprisingly effective.

THE STANCE

A. Foot Position

The toes of the back foot are aligned with the instep of the front foot keeping the feet, shoulder width apart. This enables the linemen to step with either foot first. The heels must be in line with the toes. A "heel out" emphasis or "toe in" helps the player with alignment.

B. Back Position

The back must be level with butt up and square shoulders.

C. Hand Position

The knuckles are placed on the ground on a line inside the foot. The weight must be distributed equally between the hands and feet. Weight distribution is correct when the player is not easily yanked on his face or shivered on his butt.

D. Head Position

The head is up. Linemen must be able to determine who is in their blocking area.

Note: All of our linemen take a four point stance except the center. Split ends may drop their back foot more and look to the inside.

CENTER STANCE AND SNAP

Stance

We work with right handed centers and quarterbacks only. The following description is based on this premise.

Most of our centers drop their left foot slightly. We never allow them to take more than a toe-instep relationship, however. Some boys can take a parallel stance and get off the ball and into a block quickly. There is nothing sacred about either method of foot alignment. The feet should be slightly more than shoulder width apart, however.

Diagram 11: Center stances

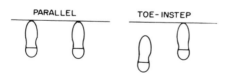

All of the center's weight is placed on the balls of his feet, not on his hands. The heels are raised slightly and are in line with the toes. The head is up, the back level and shoulders square.

Diagram 12: Heel-toe alignment

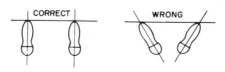

Snap

The positioning of the ball and hand placement are very important factors in consistent snaps. The ball's axis must be kept on straight parallel and perpendicular lines with the strings tilted to the left of center.

Diagram 13: Ball alignment

The right hand grasps the ball slightly foreward of center. The "V" of the thumb and forefinger should be straight. The strings strike the center's thumb. The left hand is placed near the back point of the ball to act as a guide. The shoulders are easily leveled if downward pressure is applied to the left hand.

Our centers always move with their left foot first. If a right shoulder block is necessary, the first step with the left foot is very short. Requiring this quick left foot jab, keeps the right leg from hindering the snap of the right arm.

Diagram 14: Center steps at snap

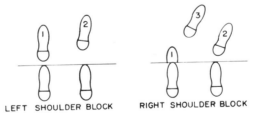

Since the center is shooting away from the quarterback with the snap, he must keep a fully extended right arm in order to reach the desired point of exchange. We want the ball fired as far back and up as possible. Normal arm and wrist rotation is all that is necessary.

One major cause of fumbles in the exchange is that the center moves his butt up or down as the snap occurs. Don't let the center jerk his head down as he snaps the ball back. This allows the butt to go up. The opposite is true if the head is jerked up at the snap.

Good centers are developed by starting them in the junior high. If the little quick boy is allowed to always play this position until J. V. ball, you will only develop an adequate center on the varsity.

LINE STANCE AND BLOCKING TECHNIQUES

Drills To Teach Stance

Diagram 15: Stance Instruction

A. Players are in a circle facing the coach. The coach checks each stance by shivering or pulling the player while in his stance

B. Players face each other and check their partner's balance while in a stance. The coach walks the line and assists

For the first two weeks, every time the players assume a stance for a drill in the shoots or on the sleds, the coach checks stances.

Blocking Techniques

One-on-one block

If a lineman is to block a man on his nose to his right, he steps with his right foot first trying to drive a knee into the crotch of this opponent and the helmet into the defender's belt buckle. The head slides to the side opposite the lead leg on contact. The blocker lifts with his head as his knees come under him. This enables him to work up on the defender. He must drive the opponent backward. The blocker should *not* swing his body into the hole.

Diagram 16: One-on-one block

Post and Power Block

The post man executes a one-on-one block. If the power blocker is on the right, the post man uses a right shoulder block, thereby, slipping his head to the left. The right foot lead by the post man will help seal the seam between him and the power blocker. Putting the post man's head on the left influences the defender to fight pressure the wrong way.

The power blocker steps with his inside foot, to seal the seam next to the post man. He drives his helmet into the defender's side in the middle of his rib cage. If the helmet is aimed in front, the defender can easily roll out of the two time. If the head goes behind, the defender can split the seam.

Diagram 17: Post and power block

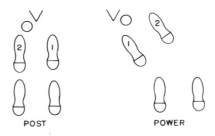

Smear Block

The smear blocking technique is used whenever a defender is in the blocker's inside gap. The blocker steps down the line with his inside foot first closing the gap. His head goes across the front of the defender. Contact is made with the outside shoulder by driving the outside leg into the defender on the second step. Putting the head in front stops the defender's penetration. On contact the blocker should attempt to drive the defender down the line and dump him over the next inside lineman.

The biggest problem in teaching this technique is getting the blocker to fire for the spot where the defender will be after the snap. Inexperienced players lunge out toward the defender's position at alignment.

This block is used mainly in short yardage situations and against goal line defenses. Since these are the crucial game situations, daily drills on this technique are necessary.

Diagram 18: Smear blocking (A defender is charging the inside gap)

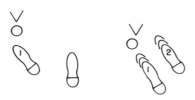

1. Step with the inside foot first
2. Throw the head down the line and across the front of the defender
3. Bring the outside foot up with a high knee
4. Raise the head and drive

Linebacker Blocking

A blocker should never go after a linebacker at his position of alignment. He should take a shallow route to a point of anticipated contact. This is a point between the linebacker and the running lane. The block is executed as a high one-on-one shoulder block driving the helmet into the numbers.

Maintaining contact with the defender is the most important element. To do this the blocker must use short choppy steps and a wide base. He should concentrate on running through the defender, trying to step on his toes. Always drive the linebacker back and go with his flow. The runner will find the daylight.

Diagram 19: Linebacker blocking

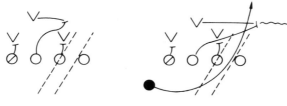

Down Field Blocking

Releasing

Release techniques must be mastered if the linemen are to be effective down field blockers. Always release inside a defender playing on a blocker. Shoot out low throwing the outside arm across the front of the defender keeping the inside hand low for support. Stay low, sprinting in a shallow path to the running lane. We stress blocking across the running lane and up it.

Diagram 20: Release paths to the running lane

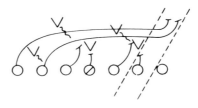

Never pass any defender to get another. Block any opponent in your field of vision.

Executing the Block

Again, the one-on-one block is used in the same manner as used on linebackers. The blocker must concentrate on getting close before he throws the block and on keeping his head in front of the defender's path of motion.

The blocker is not to leave his feet. We emphasize aiming the helmet at the numbers, but dipping the head and shoulders before contact for the pop. Maintain contact as long as possible.

3

DEVELOPING VERSATILITY IN THE BACKFIELD

STANCE

As with our linemen, the backs must be able to move with versatility in directions other than straight ahead. We have found that a two point stance does not afford enough regimentation for a high school back. We, therefore, use a three point stance for all running backs regardless of their position or set.

Halfback Stance

The halfbacks use a three point stance with their feet slightly less than shoulder width apart. The feet maintain a toe-instep relationship with the butt up, back level, and head up. Their weight rests primarily on the balls of their feet.

Fullback Stance

The fullback must move well laterally. His feet should be almost parallel and shoulder width apart. Even though his hand is down, very little weight, if any, is placed on it. Keeping the fullback down makes it difficult for the defense to key his first steps and it eliminates leaning.

BACKFIELD BLOCKING

All backs use the same block regardless of the man they are

blocking. Our backs are never assigned a block on an interior line-man. Their rules call for blocking linebackers and secondary people. The fullback often blocks on the defensive end, however.

All of the backs are instructed to hit with a high one-on-one shoulder block aiming their helmet at the numbers. To be an effective blocker, a back must get in close to the defender and "pop" up into the numbers. The "pop" block is executed by dipping the head and shoulders and dropping the butt before contact. The blocker pops out and up into the numbers. He must use a wide base and try to run through the defender. The blocker does not leave his feet. He tries to maintain contact as long as possible. We never ask a back to block a man in a certain direction, just screen him off. If the defender is moving in a sideways direction, the blocker should put his head across the front of the defender.

PASS PROTECTION BLOCKING BY BACKS

Our backs attack pass rushers. Small backs cannot stand and take blows from on-rushing two hundred pound linemen. The back has a lane to check and priorities on whom to block on pocket passes.

Diagram 21: Backfield pass protection blocking (pocket)

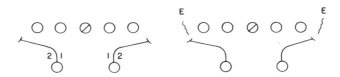

The backs block lower than normal on pass protection to bring the defenders' hands down. He aims his "pop" at the base of the numbers.

On action or sprint-out passes the backs go after their assignment but they still pop low.

QUARTERBACK FUNDAMENTALS

Every play from the line of scrimmage starts with ball handling by the quarterback. He must be comfortable, yet be in a stance that will enable him to move quickly. Our quarterbacks crowd up to the center with their feet parallel but wider than their shoulders. They keep their toes inside the center's heels, however. His knees are flexed and the back is straight.

The quarterback adjusts his hands to the center's butt. The heels of his hands must be together. The fingers are extended but not tense. The right hand is on top for a right handed boy. Unlike much theory, we do not advocate shoving the hands into the middle of the center's crotch. We have found that the quarterbacks can stand straighter and can be more relaxed if they don't bury their hands in the center's crotch. It is much easier to perform the reverse pivot if he is not in a stooped position. Therefore, our quarterback's hands are high on the center's butt. However, pressure with the knuckles is necessary so that the center can feel the hand position. This pressure is maintained throughout the exchange. A key coaching point is keeping the quarterback's elbows flexed.

Mistakes will happen if the quarterback pulls away too soon. He must be forced to maintain the pressure of the top hand by following the center with his arms as the snap occurs.

Diagram 22: Quarterback stance

Setting the Ball

After the snap, the quarterback should have the ball firmly implanted in both hands with the strings against the top fingers. He must automatically "set" the ball next. The set is accomplished by placing the point of the ball in his stomach. If he doesn't set the ball, he will have a tendency to swing it up into the runner's pocket rather than jab it at a level from belt buckle to belt buckle.

Diagram 23: Setting the ball and handing off

Pivoting

Like many teams that use a multiple offense, we run some basic split "T" belly plays that require the quarterback to open up to the ball carrier immediately, but the main maneuver required of him is to execute the reverse pivot.

We ran our present offense for two years without the reverse pivot and then two years with the pivot. There is no doubt that the trapping game is much more effective with the reverse pivot. The ball is hidden from most of the defense as soon as the quarterback turns. The linebackers and secondary men must then key movement and flow, not quarterback action.

To execute a pivot, the quarterback turns on the foot to the side he is going, but he reverses out by turning his left hip out if he is going to move right. The degree of turn on the pivot and the depth on the turn varies according to the demands of each play.

Diagram 24: Reverse pivot to right

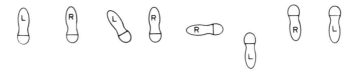

Handoffs

We ask the quarterback to jam the ball at the runner, never swing it up! Usually both hands are on the ball. The runner is required to make a pocket with his inside elbow at chin height. The bottom elbow is held slightly away from the body. The ball should be jammed through to the runner's far hip. When a faking back does not get the ball, he is to continue his fake five yards beyond the line of scrimmage.

Diagram 25: Handoff

4

TEACHING FUNDAMENTALS OF SPLIT LINE PLAY

RULES FOR SPLITTING THE LINE

Rule I

We split the line to spread the defense. If the splits create natural holes in the defense and help isolate a defensive man, there will be daylight for the runner.

We do not split to get angles because we don't feel they are necessary. We prefer that the defensive man is taken back. However, if the defense stays tight, blocking angles will result. By splitting, we create the running room. Our blockers only have to occupy the defensive man where he is or drive him back. If linemen are taught to get blocking angles, they will swing their butts into the holes and interfere with the runner.

Rule II

Our linemen are given minimum and maximum alternatives for their splits. The guards' splits are from one and a half to two feet, tackles two to three feet and ends two and a half feet out.

As a basic rule the guards and tackles take maximum splits versus an even defense and minimum versus an odd defense. An even set is recognized by the alignment of two defensive men playing on the head of the guards. An odd alignment is defined as no men on the guards' head, but a man on the center's nose.

Diagram 26: Even-odd alignment

If the defense plays an even set head up, the offensive man can maneuver him away from the play. If they are playing a set distance from the defensive man next to them, the offense can split and angles will result.

Diagram 27: Set distance-defense play

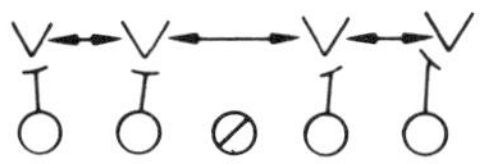

The daylight is already created when running against the odd defense, but the danger is from the "red dog." Taking a minimum split enables the offense to cut off the crashing linebacker. The guards step with their inside foot first when the "red dog" is apparent.

Rule III

The third basic rule that alters the line splits is *always take minimum splits versus a "do-dad" or a gap defense.* The offensive line must close down when the defense is lined up to penetrate inside seams. A "do-dad" is merely a tandem set with the linebacker up close to crash. Whenever a lineman recognizes this deal in his blocking area, he gives a check call that tells the next lineman to his outside (play side if he is the center) to block down and help on the do-dad. The smear blocking technique is used with the head going across the front of the charging defender.

Diagram 28: Blocking a do-dad from minimum splits
Step with the inside foot, head across the front of the man coming into the blocker's face.

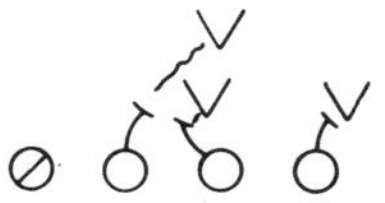

The same splitting and blocking techniques are used against the gap defense. If a defensive man is lined up in a gap, the blocker is instructed to close down so that he covers half the defender.
Diagram 29: Blocking a man in the gap

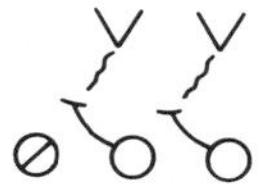

Step with the inside foot first, head across the front.

Rule IV

When executing a post and power block, the power man is to take a minimum split. This enables the power blocker to reach the defender quickly and close his inside seam with his inside lead step thereby, preventing the defender from cracking through.

Rule V

All releasers take maximum splits. To get down field and block, the releaser must have running room. He wants to blast off the line of scrimmage and not be interfered with. Splitting out will allow him more room to get clear right now at the snap.
Diagram 30: Split to release

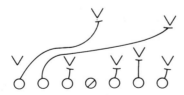

The lineman's biggest problem is maintaining his splits. During group work, we have one coach check splits every time the team lines up. He doesn't step in and discuss the split with a player, but he quickly moves him in or out or just points to the lineman's feet to make him aware of his split.

In summary our linemen split to spread the defense. Maximum splits are taken against even defenses and when releasing. Minimum splits are used when facing odd defenses, gap defenses and do-dads and when power blocking in a two-on-one situation.

LINING UP ON THE BALL

Proper alignment at the line of scrimmage is imperative in split line play. If every man bows back a little, the team has lost a yard before the snap of the ball. Because the linemen do split out, it becomes extremely difficult for the players to tell whether or not they are on line. However, this fault can be corrected but only with proper teaching. Just yelling at a player now and then will not correct this problem.

Our center breaks early from the huddle, and takes his position over the ball. The other linemen then break the huddle and take a semi-erect stance at the line (hands on knees, head up). They are only six inches apart at this point. The guards line up with their toes even with the center's heels. The tackles and ends line up toe to toe with the guards.

Diagram 31: Alignment at line of scrimmage

CENTER   GUARD   TACKLE   END

At the command "set" the linemen move laterally to their outside, picking up their outside foot first. They practice keeping their feet in line as they extend. This movement at the line serves a twofold purpose. It enables them to adjust their splits according to the defensive set and helps them keep on line. As the season progresses, they are able to spread more while in an upright position.

In assuming their stance the linemen should place their hands on the ground immediately, then adjust their feet with a slight backward movement. If they are allowed to move backward first, they lose their depth perspective. Using this technique, they will have a tendency to encroach the neutral zone rather than sway back.

To check their line position, the guards look to their inside and adjust so that they are peering into the center's shoulder pad. The tackles and ends check inside and adjust on a sight line even with the next man's helmet.

In the first two weeks of practice all plays are run on lines so that the linemen know what they are to see when they check alignment from their down position. A manager is also assigned to check alignment in drills and scrimmage. The quarterback always checks his line after the command "set." He is instructed to tell the players to move up or back if they are out of position.

Using a manager and chalk lines combined with the flexing movement on the line at the start of the season should impress the players enough that they become proud of their formation. We usually shoot a roll of 8mm film the first week of practice on huddles, huddle breaks, alignment and stance. Pride in being sharp on these facets of the game is real important and is worth a roll of film.

A unique problem in alignment is the split end. We have a split end on most plays. If he lines up in the backfield or over the ball, it is a five yard penalty. He is the last man down on the line. He must check to his inside just as if he were in tight. The quarterback assists him verbally if needed. We do require the end to go into a down stance. If he stands up, he might find alignment easier, but there is a greater danger of movement or lean from a standing position. Also we have found that ends are much slower in reacting from the standing position. We follow the same philosophy in the formations in our kicking game.

FIRE OUT AT THE SNAP

Whatever cadence you like, that is the one to use if your team is successful with it. We believe in a non-rhythmic count. Our players always anticipated the cadence in a rhythmic count. They seem to build up and explode more crisply from the non-cadence count. After the command "set," the quarterback gives our check-off calls. Then he yells "Ready—hike." This tells the players to be ready to charge on the next sound. They fire out on "Go!" We sometimes fire on the second "Go" or even on "Ready—hike" just to keep the defense honest.

5

DEFINING BLOCKING PRINCIPLES

The best blocking system is a simple one. In our system each player has a rule that designates an order of precedence as to which man he is to block in his area. All regular plays fit the basic rule. Before memorizing this rule, the players must understand the terminology used in the rule.

TERMINOLOGY FOR BLOCKING RULES

Gap rule

Block any man on the line of scrimmage between me and the first man to my inside.
Diagram 32: Gap rule

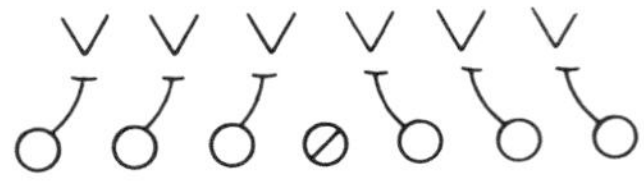

Inside rule

Block the first man to my inside. This also includes the man who plays head on the man to my inside.
Diagram 33: Inside rule

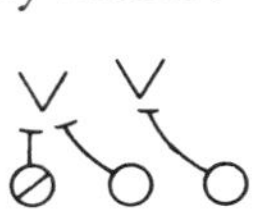

Over rule

Block line backers over my area. A linebacker is any man that doesn't have his hand on the ground. This includes any linebacker from my area to the center.

Diagram 34: Over rule

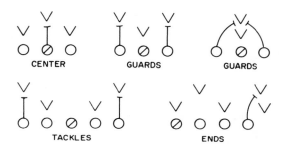

On rule

Block the man on my nose.

Diagram 35: On rule

Outside rule

Block the first lineman to my outside.

Diagram 36: Outside rule

Lane rule

Release to the running lane—block across it and up field.

Diagram 37: Lane rule

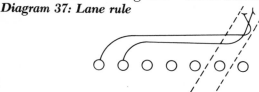

Rules for the center only

> *Backside*—block the first lineman to my backside.
> *Frontside*—block the first lineman to my frontside.
> *L.B. backside*—block the first line backer to my backside.

Diagram 38: Center rules

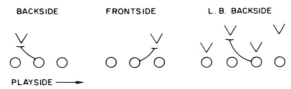

The smear technique is used when blocking a player on the backside or frontside.

THE REGULAR BLOCKING RULE

The regular rule is explained here before the trap rule because in teaching our blocking system we always attempt to have the players gain a complete understanding of the basic application of the terminology before any variations are interjected.

Once the player learns the order of precedence for the "regular rule" he always follows that rule on the basic plays. The rule simply designates which area over the player he is to block first. If a defensive player is in that area, he is to get him. If there is no man in the first area, the player blocks any man in the next area of priority.

Regular rule

> *Center*—on-over-lane
> *Guard and tackle*—gap-on-over-outside
> *End*—on-over-inside L.B.-inside
> *Backs*—first back at the hole—over-L.B. inside: second back at the hole—outside-L.B. outside

Diagram 39: Regular rule—center play

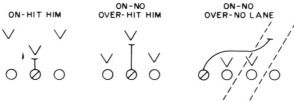

Diagram 40: Regular rule—guard and tackle play

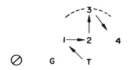

As the guards and tackles approach the line of scrimmage, they check their gap first. If a defensive player is lined up in it, they get him. Their next priority is "on." If a man is on their nose, they block him. If they have no man in their gap or on their nose, they check "over" for a linebacker. In other words, the blocker checks from his inside to his outside for any defensive players in his area. The first man he comes to, he blocks.

Diagram 41: Regular rule—end play

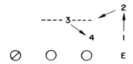

The ends have a different order of precedence than the guards and tackles. The ends look straight ahead first, not inside. His eyes follow the path of arrows above.

Lane Blocking

We still feel some players can release to the running lane in high school even though the backs are to run for daylight. Our linemen perform a block at the line of scrimmage only when the hole called is within two holes of his numbered position or on his side of the line. If the play is farther away, he releases to the running lane. The guards, however, would never release if a man was playing on his nose. The center's rule automatically takes care of all his release situations.

Backfield blocking—regular rule

Usually backs have blocking assignments on off tackle or power plays. The first blocking back to reach the hole blocks the "over" area. The second blocking back at the hole hits any defensive player outside the offensive end.

Diagram 42: Regular rule—backfield play

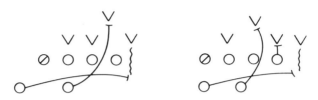

NUMBERING SYSTEM

We use nine digits numbering from right to left.

Diagram 43: Numbering system

Numbers 1 and 9 designate the sweep areas. The off-tackle areas are 2 and 8. These are not exact holes in game situations, but they do indicate an explicit area for the back to turn up into. The 3 and 7 areas are the least variable. These numbers are used mainly to indicate dive holes. Areas 4 and 6 indicate which side of center the play will break. The 5 area is applied to the center area.

There are many suitable numbering systems. We have found this one effectively serves our needs. We don't like to use the same numbers on each side of the line and then call "right" and "left" in the huddle. We, thereby, reserve the terms "right" and "left" for backfield sets and special directions such as "flanker left."

The ball carrier is designated by calling his position with the hole number. A sample call is "lefthalf at 2" or "fullback at 4."

Diagram 44: Play calls—fullback at 4

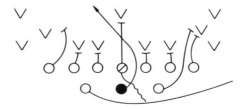

SUMMARY

All blocking on basic plays must fit whatever "regular rule" is devised. The only other rules a lineman will have to learn will be for special plays. To indicate a special play, the quarterback adds a word key to the call in the huddle. The blocker may have to apply a new order of precedence for the special play but the terminology stays the same. Some of these exceptions to the basic rule are trap plays and pitches for the sweep. The remainder of this book will deal with the trapping game only.

II

Executing Running Trap Plays

No matter what formation or series is used, only one rule is needed for a team to run the short trap, and one rule to run the off tackle trap. Variations of backfield maneuvers can be applied, or the ball carrier may be changed, but the basic blocking rule must remain constant. No high school team has time to master two or three separate blocking formulas for a trap play.

It has been our experience that we can run the short trap and the long trap well if we teach each play to one side of the line only. Usually a team only has one fast guard that can pull for the longer off-tackle trap. If our breakaway runner is the left half, we place the fastest guard at left guard so that we can run the off tackle to the right. Adversely, if we run the off tackle trap to the right, we run the short trap to the left so as to keep balance in our running attack.

As the season progresses, we may add another trap play if the team has the ability to master the execution. The main coaching point is don't attempt more than the team can perform at the start of the season. We believe in expertise on one trap first rather than average execution on two or three.

6

PERFECTING THE SHORT TRAP RULE ASSIGNMENTS

SHORT TRAP RULE

FSE—over-L.B. outside-lane
FST—L.B. inside-outside
FSG—inside-outside
C—backside-on
BSG—trap in
BSE—lane
BST—gap-on-over-outside
Back—First back or slot back-L.B. outside-lane

Regardless of the backfield maneuvers, this one rule is the only formula the line uses in blocking the short trap. Once the line learns to execute this rule properly, any number of formations and plays can be run in the backfield at the hole.

For simplicity the plays will be drawn to one side only. Our holes are so numbered that the short trap to the left is called the "6 trap." Below is an application of the "6 trap" rule against various defenses.

NOTE ON TANDEM SET BLOCKING

The front side tackle is taught to take the man that charges into his face as he looks to the outside. The trapper hits the first man

Diagrams 45: 6 trap rule

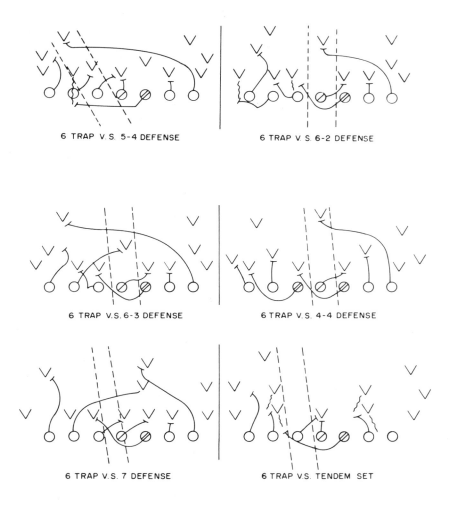

6 TRAP V.S. 5-4 DEFENSE

6 TRAP V.S. 6-2 DEFENSE

6 TRAP V.S. 6-3 DEFENSE

6 TRAP V.S. 4-4 DEFENSE

6 TRAP V.S. 7 DEFENSE

6 TRAP V.S. TENDEM SET

past the center that comes to his face. The backside tackle seals his inside gap.

TEACHING THE SHORT TRAP

The rule designates whom the player is to block, but he must still learn how to block his man. The following discussion will clarify the techniques each player is to use.

FRONTSIDE END PLAY—6 TRAP
(OVER—L.B. OUTSIDE-LANE)

The left end is the frontside end on the 6 trap. Against most standard defenses, his job is to cut off the outside linebacker from the running lane. (See diagram of 6 trap vs. 5-4, 6-2, 6-3 defenses.) If the linebacker is playing wide, he has no problem. However, if the linebacker is on his nose keying the on-side back, the end's job is more difficult. The further in the linebacker plays, the sharper the angle the end must take to get between that linebacker and the running lane.

Diagram 46: Front side end play—6 trap rule

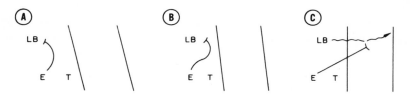

In diagram B the end steps with his inside foot first and drives down the line taking a shallow path toward the running lane. No matter what, the end must make contact with the defender and stay on his feet. The end should try to step on the linebacker's toes as he blocks him. If the linebacker runs laterally (diagram C) he must run with him. Keep the defender occupied. It is up to the back to cut and find daylight.

Many times the scout report will alter the end's play. If the defense is playing their end soft so that he doesn't cross the line of scrimmage and is thereby causing trouble on 6 counter traps, the end may have to block him. When this happens, we simply tell our end to block the opponent's defensive end on the 6 counter trap. We would run drills on this change throughout the week and make it part of our game plan if the scout report had picked up this maneuver.

The soft end would close down and start a line of pursuit because his key (the on-side back) is moving away from him. Since the tackle has an inside linebacker to block, the defensive end is free to make the tackle unless our offensive end picks him up. To make the block, the end takes one step to the inside and turns. This step gives him time to check the area visually. He then blasts the closest de-

Diagram 47: Blocking soft end play—6 counter trap

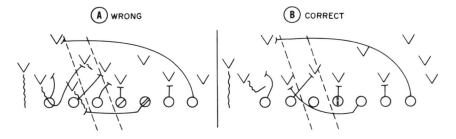

fender to his outside which will be the soft end in this case (diagram B).

This adjustment is made only when the defense has an inside linebacker in combination with soft end play. The standard rule handles soft end play in all other situations.

FRONTSIDE TACKLE PLAY—6 TRAP
(L.B. INSIDE-OUTSIDE)

L.B. inside

If there is a linebacker in an area from over him to the center, he must block him. To perform the block effectively he must stay on his feet. Our linemen block all linebackers the easy way, but with their head in front of the movement. The tackle should run the linebacker across the running lane. This block presents no problem on counter traps.

Diagram 48: Tackle block on linebacker—6 counter trap

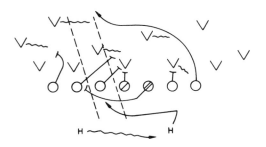

The tackle blocks with his head in front of the flow.

If the backfield movement is toward the 6 hole, the tackle has a real tough job. His head will still have to go in front of the movement. He must go low on any crashing linebacker.

Diagram 49: Tackle block on linebacker—6 trap

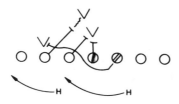

In some stunting defenses a pinching defensive player will cut the tackle off from the center linebacker. In this case, he will have to take an outside route to get to the linebacker.

Diagram 50: Tackle block on linebacker—6 trap (outside route)

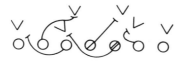

Outside rule

When there is no inside linebacker, the tackle blocks outside. This means he hits the first man on the line of scrimmage outside the offensive end.

Diagram 51: Tackle block—6 trap (outside)

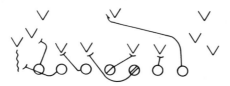

The outside influence of the guard and tackle greatly increases the effectiveness of the play. As a defender checks to his outside, he is hit with an inside-out block. It should be noted that the tackle's head is on the inside of the end cutting him off from a direct pursuit angle.

Note: All linemen put their heads on the inside when blocking out. Their heads go across the front of the defender when blocking in.

FRONTSIDE GUARD PLAY—6 TRAP (INSIDE-OUTSIDE)

The terms in the guard's rule, inside-outside, apply only to men on the line of scrimmage in a stance.

Inside rule

When blocking an odd front, there will be a defender on the center's nose. This is the "inside" man. The guard must step with his inside foot first closing his inside seam. If a post and power block is in effect, he drives his helmet into the side of the defender as the center post blocks. Communication must take place between the center and guard so that the guard knows if the center will be posting. Usually this information can be exchanged as they break the huddle, but if the defense is changing sets, a call can be made at the line of scrimmage. The center can simply say "yes" or "no." Any word call system can be devised between the two blockers involved.
Diagram 52: Frontside guard play—6 trap (inside rule)

The center post blocks with a left foot lead step. His head slips to the right. The guard power blocks stepping with his right foot first driving his head into the defender's rib cage.

When the center is unable to act as a post man, the guard gets the defender by himself. A smear blocking technique is used placing the head across the front of the defender to stop penetration.
Diagram 53: Frontside guard play—6 trap (inside rule)

The guard steps with his inside foot first. He must go down the line to get his head across the front of the defender.

Outside rule

When there is no man on the center, the frontside guard blocks the first man to his outside that is on the line of scrimmage. His first step should be directly down the line with his outside foot as if he were pulling in that direction. The second step is up into the line. He blocks the first man in his face. The head is driven into the belt buckle, but he works up immediately as if blocking a linebacker. The head is slipped to the hole side. This movement to the outside influences the defensive guard over him to follow his head to the outside, thereby setting the defender up for the trap.

Diagram 54: Frontside guard play—6 trap (outside block)

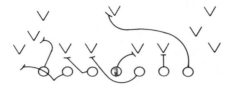

CENTER PLAY—6 TRAP (BACKSIDE-ON)

Because of the simple check system used with the guard (see frontside guard rule), we are able to use "backside-on" as the center's rule. We feel this is safer and more effective than "on-backside." However, either rule can present some unique problems against some defenses. It is immediately evident that we don't always get a post and power block on the inside of the trap. We feel the backfield movement more than compensates for this, however.

Diagram 55: Center play—6 trap (backside rule)

In diagram "B" the center gives the frontside guard a word key that calls off the post and power block. The guard must then "smear block" the defender on the center's nose.

In performing a "backside" assignment, the center blocks any defender on the line of scrimmage playing over the pulling guard. In order to cut the defender off, he must get his head across in front of the charger. We teach the center to reach across the defender with his far side arm. This move takes a lot of work. Certainly the center can't get the job done by standing up. Small quick guards will not penetrate on big slow centers if the center is taught to aim for the belt buckle and reach. The first step must be with the foot to the side he is going. This does not present any problems on the snap if the center has been taught proper stance and movement (see chapter 1—center stance and snap).

When faced with crashing linebackers, the center is instructed to play them as if they were "backside." Usually the scout report will tell if the linebackers crash from their 5-4 or 4-4 sets. For instance, they may have a tendency to crash on first down. If we expect this, we tell the center to play all center area linebackers as "backside." Never leave the center guessing. He is told to either block the linebackers as backside or not to block them. Drill periods in practice are used to make this point clear each week.

Diagram 56: Center play—6 trap (backside rule)

CRASHING LINEBACKERS

As a double check, the pulling guard uses a word key to signal the center when he is to cover for the pull.

On rule

The center posts when he has a man "on" with no "backside" responsibility. The post block is performed with a "near foot—near shoulder" techique leading with the foot on the power side so as to close the seam. After contact, his head goes low on the side opposite the power man.

Diagram 57: Center play—6 trap (on rule)

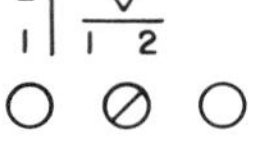

BACKSIDE GUARD PLAY—6 TRAP (TRAP IN)

The guard's alignment must be correct or he will not get precise timing on his pull. In lining up toe to heel with the center and no closer than a foot and a half away, the guard can step simultaneously with the center and pull swinging his head in without bumping the center.

Diagram 58: Backside guard play—6 trap (alignment—first step)

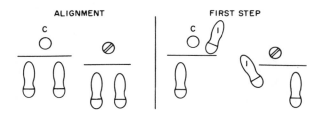

The guards first step is a short jab step toward the center. On a short trap play, the guard makes only a quarter turn on the first step. He looks "in" over the spot where the center was before the snap. His assignment is to block the first defender past the center, so he must be facing in and be ready to hit on his second step.

Step number two is in a path running at a forty-five degree angle into the line. He blocks any defender in his face. The block is made on the defensive man's inside with the guard's head on the inside. Contact is made with a pop into the belt buckle, but he is to work up right now! Short choppy steps are necessary for good balance at this point.

Diagram 59: Backside guard play—6 trap (second step and contact)

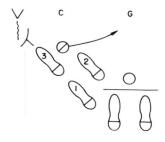

When blocking an odd front, he may have to pull all the way to the defensive tackle. On an even front, he may meet the defender on the second step. Therefore, balance is more important than speed.

Diagram 60: Backside guard play—6 trap (odd front)

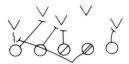

The same pattern is run even though the trapper must take more steps to reach the defender. We want the guard up in the line of scrimmage, not along it. His inside arm should brush the butts of the center and the guard. He then rounds out to meet the tackle with an inside-out block.

If any man breaks through or a linebacker crashes unexpectedly, the guard is in good position to block as long as he pulls correctly.

Diagram 61: Backside guard play—6 trap (pulling form)

One unique situation is presented when blocking the Notre Dame 4-4 defense. The line rules still work, but the backside guard actually traps a linebacker. This is no new problem because the guard has been taught to step in and block the first uncovered man past the center.

Diagram 62: Backside guard play—6 trap (trapping a linebacker)

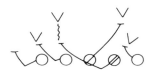

BACKSIDE TACKLE PLAY—6 TRAP
(GAP-ON-OVER-OUTSIDE)

This tackle doesn't have any change from his regular rule. He must perform his block at the line of scrimmage however. He can't release because the running lane usually passes behind his position. The counter traps are slightly delayed also. The defensive tackle is always blocked on the 6 trap.

Diagram 63: Backside tackle play—6 trap

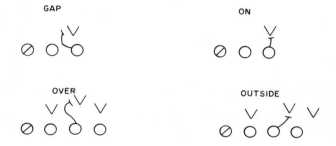

BACKSIDE END PLAY—6 TRAP (LANE)

The end releases staying close to the line. As he enters the center area, he checks for any defender to block. Sometimes he must help on a linebacker, but his usual target is the safety or far side half.

Diagram 64: Backside end play—6 trap (release to lane)

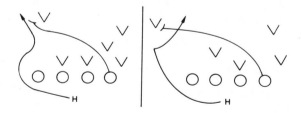

The runner should assist in setting up the block then cut for daylight.

7

TEACHING PLAY VARIETY WITH THE SHORT TRAP

A multiplicity of plays may be run at one short trap hole once the line has mastered the blocking procedure. We like to have a short trap play from every formation and series that we use.

The short trap may be run as a flow trap moving in the same direction as the pursuit or as a counter trap moving against the flow of pursuit and as a reverse play or draw play.

COUNTERFLOW TRAPS

Fullback counter traps

The short trap with the fullback carrying the ball is the most common trap play used by a majority of teams. The fullback at 6 counter trap is our favorite short trap. The flow of the defensive pursuit should be established before the counter trap is used. We set the play up with a power series using the full house "T." After running all three backs off left or right tackle a few times, we start the same movement but the fullback breaks the opposite way.

The right half runs his regular blocking path at the outside linebacker while the left half fakes his off-tackle run. The fullback also starts to the right by stepping with his right foot first. On the third

Diagram 65: Fullback at 6 counter trap ("T" formation)

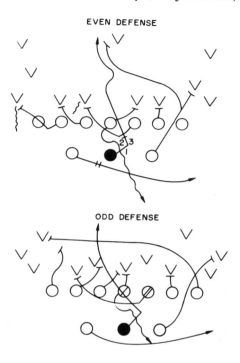

step he plants his right foot and cuts a quarter turn pointing up over the 6 hole. A cross-over step may be used by the fullback to gain better timing with some individuals. Since this is an inside handoff, the fullback will have his left elbow up.

As the quarterback executes a reverse pivot, he looks at the left half and makes a fake handoff. He then hands the ball off on his inside with his left hand. Work is needed to make this a continuous smooth movement.

The reverse pivot by the quarterback helps the effectiveness of the play. If he just opens up with the ball, the defense will not be as likely to move with the flow of the ball. Defenses are often frozen on the sight of the ball. The reverse pivot hides the ball, thereby causing the defense to react on their normal keys.

The reverse pivot also aids the trapper on his block. When the quarterback turns holding the ball in front of an unblocked defensive guard, the defender usually sells out. He then becomes an easy victim for the trapper.

Diagram 66: Quarterback reverse pivot—6 counter trap

The running backs stay fairly erect on trap plays because the hole breaks at various spots along the line against different defenses. The back can adjust more easily if he runs under control. We tell the back to run at the void spot indicated by the defensive alignment. When picking the hole, he should favor the post and power or angle block, not the trap block.

This play is equally effective from the full house "I" or triangle "I."

Diagram 67: Fullback at 6 counter trap ("I" formations)

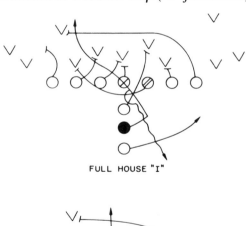

FULL HOUSE "I"

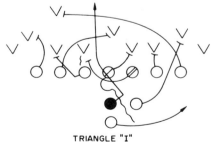

TRIANGLE "I"

We also use this play in a flanker series with the fakes going toward the flanker or away from him.

Diagram 68A: Fullback at 6 counter trap (wing "T")

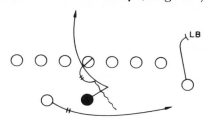

Diagram 68B: Fullback at 6 counter trap (wing "T" with motion)

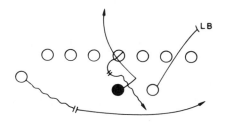

This same trap play is very effective with the belly series, too. Because defenses key the first movement of the quarterback so well in the belly series, a quick hitting counter is needed to keep the linebackers honest. The fullback at 6 counter trap does this.

Diagram 69: Fullback at 6 counter trap (belly series)

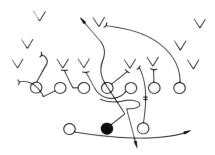

The quarterback need not make a good fake to the diving half, but he should show the ball to the defense. He takes two steps, plants his left foot and pivots back. He hands off with his right hand.

The fullback will not need to go far to his right, but he may have to delay slightly.

HALFBACK COUNTER TRAPS

There is also a variety of halfback plays possible with the short trap. Again the counter is effective in cutting down on defensive pursuit.

Diagram 70: Right half at 6 counter trap

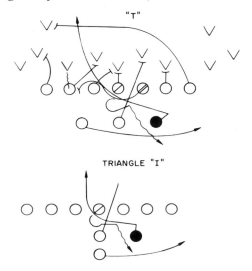

The crossing action of the fullback hides the counter movement of the half. This play works especially well against a 5-4 or 4-4 front that is crashing linebackers. The fullback can pick up any defensive penetration on the back side of the play.

The simplest footwork for the right half is a short jab step with the left foot, step and plant the right foot and cut. He can vary his alignment to gain correct timing at the handoff. Because of the distance the half travels to the hole, the play is slower in developing than the fullback counter trap. The advantage is that the flow of pursuit is greater.

HALFBACK DIVE TRAP

The quicker hitting right half at 6 dive trap may be used if more speed is desired in the halfback trap. If not flanked, the fullback goes behind the half in a regular belly pattern. The quarterback opens up facing the diving back, but he must come back off the line of scrimmage to meet the half. The right half lines up a little deeper and cheats toward the center so that he can make the cut after he receives the ball. His first step is ahead, but slanting toward the hole slightly.

Diagram 71: Right half at 6 dive trap

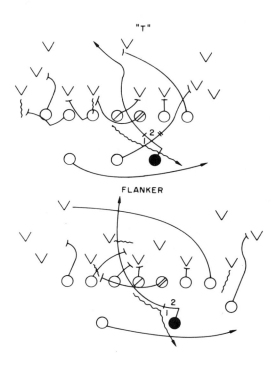

WING REVERSE TRAP

All offenses using a wing or flanker set need a reverse of some type to balance the defensive rotation or monster keys. If the wing reverse is carried too deep, it is easily detected. A reverse by the wingback around the far side tackle or end takes too long to develop. Running the wing reverse up into the short trap hole makes it a quick hitting reverse because of the shorter distance to the hole and the inside handoff.

By setting the wing a little deeper than normal from the line of scrimmage and cheating him in slightly, he will have a short straight path to the hole.

To start this play the quarterback executes a reverse pivot and fakes a pitch to the halfback or tailback as on a power sweep. In the same motion he hands the ball off on his inside to the wingback. All backs start with the snap of the ball. No delay steps are needed.

Diagram 72: Wing reverse at 6 trap

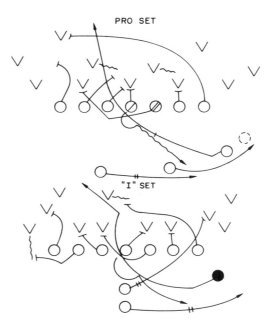

This is a good third down and long yardage play. The defensive right linebacker may be pulled out of the play by splitting the left end. In order to get double coverage on the split end, the defense must loosen up at the corners or shift opposite the power. The threat of a reverse in the middle plus a split end to cover will keep the defense from over shifting for the power plays run toward the wing.

If this play is run from the "I," the fullback may run a path in front of the wing, thereby hiding the wing's reverse action. After running the wing reverse a few times in a game, some teams bring the wing back on a fake reverse and carry out the sweep or sprint out pass.

FLOW TRAPS

Thus far all of the short traps described hit against the flow of the pursuing defensive players. Many times it is more advantageous to hit in behind the interior pursuit. In a trap play of this type the backs move in the same direction as the puller. The right half at 6 trap is a good flow trap play. This play may be run from the belly series with a ride to the fullback or from a pitch series.

Diagram 73: Right half at 6 trap (belly series, fullback fake)

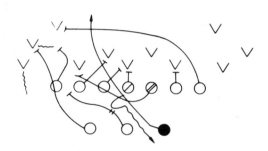

In the ride series the quarterback makes a reverse pivot and rides the fullback one step. He then steps back and hands the ball to the backside half. He should always continue his fake back away from the line to keep from being hit after the handoff.

The fullback steps with his left foot first. He plants it and drives up over the 7 hole. On all fakes requiring a ride, the fullback should place his inside elbow at chin level and fake down over the ball with an exaggerated motion.

The backside half steps to the left with the left foot first. He plants this foot and cuts up off the rear of the trapping guard. Even if the defense is over shifting to the wing or triangle "I" set and keying their center linebackers on the fullback's movement, this play will go when the tailback is used as the runner.

Riding the fullback at the defensive guard on an even line keeps the guard concentrating on the fake coming at him, making the trapper's job easier and the hole wider.

The tailback can fake either way at the snap depending upon the fakes of the other plays in the series or the linebacker's keys.

Diagram 74: Tailback at 6 trap (fullback ride) vs. an over-shifted defense

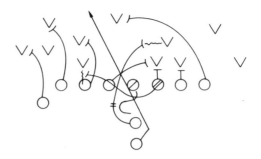

Diagram 75: Tailback at 6 trap (fullback ride) even defense

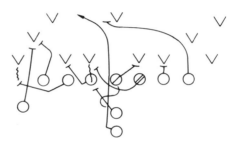

We make only one change when running this play with a quick pitch fake. The fullback runs a path toward the end as on the sweep if we are in an "I." He is usually flankered, however.

Diagram 76: Right half at 6 trap (pitch fake)

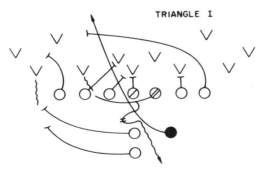

FLANKER SERIES

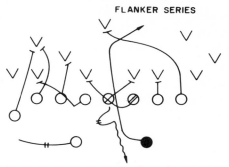

We have had greater success in our trap plays off the pitch fake since the quarterback has been using the reverse pivot. He can see the runner from the moment the ball is snapped. His timing is much better now and we never miss on the hand back as we did sometimes when the quarterback opened up to the play and stepped down the line.

If we desire more speed on the 6 hole flow trap, the play is called right half at 6 fast trap. On this play no fake is made before

Diagram 77: Right half at 6 fast trap

EVEN

ODD

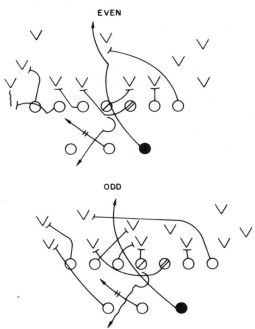

the handoff. Instead of faking a ride to the fullback or a pitch to the left half, the quarterback opens up to the right half who dives directly at the 6 hole. No side step or delay is used. The handoff is made immediately as the quarterback reverses out. We have him get depth on his first step with the right foot so as to clear the running lane fast. As he pulls his left leg out of the way, he hands off with his left hand on the inside. He continues on out to the left side of the line after the handoff.

The right half steps toward the 6 hole with his left foot first and receives the ball on his second step with his left elbow up. He plants his left foot on the third step and turns up into the hole.

The other backs fake a power play to the left when in the "T." The play is effective from any formation.

The right half may cheat up and in to gain speed. He can hit the line as soon as the trapper crosses the running lane.

DRAW PLAYS

The draw play is a very necessary and effective part of every offense. The draw can be used in almost any situation where there is an anticipated rush from the forcing unit of the defense. Since the draw is used when the defense is charging, blocking it with trapping action makes the play especially effective.

The quarterback comes straight back two steps holding the ball chest high with his shoulders turned to the right. The fullback steps to the right to set up for a pass block. He lifts his left elbow as the quarterback lowers the ball and slips it to the fullback as he turns to retreat for more depth.

Diagram 78: Fullback at 6 trap draw

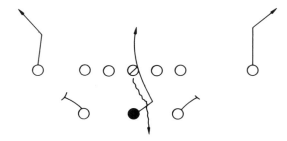

The quarterback drops back continuing a pass fake after the handoff.

The draw works well in a definite pass situation. Splitting the ends and flankering a back spreads the defense and increases the effectiveness of the draw.

The right half at 6 trap draw may be run from either sprintout or drop-back action.

Diagram 79: Right half at 6 trap draw

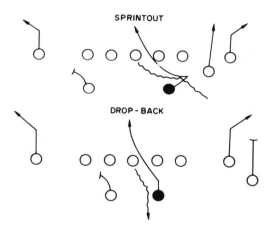

Experimentation with timing is important on draw plays. As the quarterback sprints toward the corner on the sprintout draw, the right half sets up for a pass block. He forms a pocket just as the quarterback reaches him. The same action is simulated on the drop-back draw. The quarterback carries the ball in both hands chest high while sprinting to the half who is standing in his blocking position.

The quarterback action is the important factor in a successful draw play. He should not hold the ball over his head in an unusual fashion or back peddle in a different manner than normal. We teach him to hold the ball in both hands as he retreats to a point just in front of the ball carrier. He is to look up field at the receivers as he drops back. When he reaches the handoff point, he looks the ball into the pocket of the waiting back as on a regular handoff.

SUMMARY

Short Trap

It is not necessary to teach the short trap to both sides of the line. Enough variety may be obtained by running various backfield maneuvers from many formations at the same hole in the line. If a defense is set to stop the short trap, it will jam both sides of the line.

The linemen have only to learn one rule in order to trap all defenses.

The counter trap is effective against a fast pursuing team. The wing reverse into the short trap hole helps to discourage the over shifting of defenses to meet power sets. Short traps can be used to hit in behind the flow of a fast pursuing defensive unit. Lastly, the short trap is especially effective when used to block the draw.

The play of the defensive guard or guards never determines the strategy of how or when to run the short trap. We never expect to do more than hold the trapped defender to a stand off. Whether he charges, floats, turns in or out makes no difference as long as the puller ties him up momentarily.

The back is taught to run close to the two-time or angle block. He must have his weight under control to hit the opening properly because the hole opens at different spots depending on the defensive sets.

When using the short trap against red-dogging linebackers, it is safer and often more effective to use a scissors action leading the fullback into the backside to pick up any crashers.

8

PERFECTING THE LONG TRAP RULE ASSIGNMENTS

Like the short trap rule, the long trap rule remains the same regardless of the backfield maneuvers. We use the long trap from all of our formations. In our numbering system the long trap to the right is called the 3 trap. We only put this trap in on the right side to start the season. Usually this is all we can accomplish in a year. If a team can run the long trap to one side of the line and the short trap to the other, they will have an effective inside trapping game.

LONG TRAP RULE

FSE—LB inside
FST—inside-inside linebacker
FSG—inside-on
   C—backside-on-over
BSG—trap in
BST—lane
BSE—lane
Backs—first or slot back—LB outside—lane

Diagram 80 shows some examples of the 3 trap rule against a few basic defenses.

Diagram 80: 3 trap rule

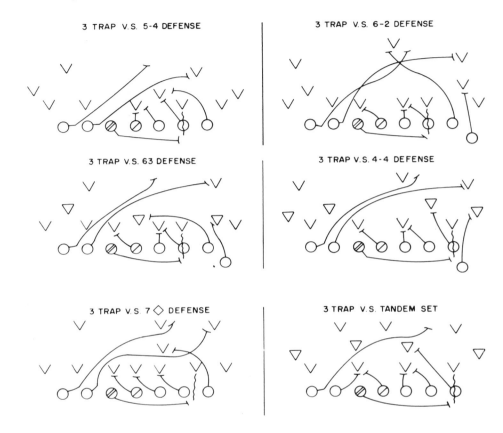

TEACHING THE LONG TRAP

The following discussion explains the rule by position and covers the techniques used to perform each block. We feel that this trap is the most effective play in our system. We build our other plays around it. Any series we run will have a 3 trap in it off the basic faking maneuver used in that series. As soon as the line has a fair concept of the regular rule, we start teaching the 3 trap rule.

Frontside end play—3 trap (LB inside)

The right end is on the front side of our 3 trap. His rule, linebacker inside, means he must block the first linebacker on his inside.

He is taught to keep his feet on the block and screen the defender off from the running lane. He should aim chest high on the block, use short choppy steps at contact and work up trying to step on the linebacker's toes.

The end must get down the line in a hurry in order to keep the linebacker from entering the running lane. If he steps with his inside foot and takes a shallow path down the line, he will get to the blocking area in time to perform his assignment.

Because the linebackers are reading their keys and flowing with the movement of the backs, they are often taken by surprise on this block making it a devastating hit.

If there is no inside linebacker, the end still blocks across the area and then up field taking the first defender to cross his face so as to seal the inside of the running lane.

Diagram 81: Frontside end play—3 trap rule

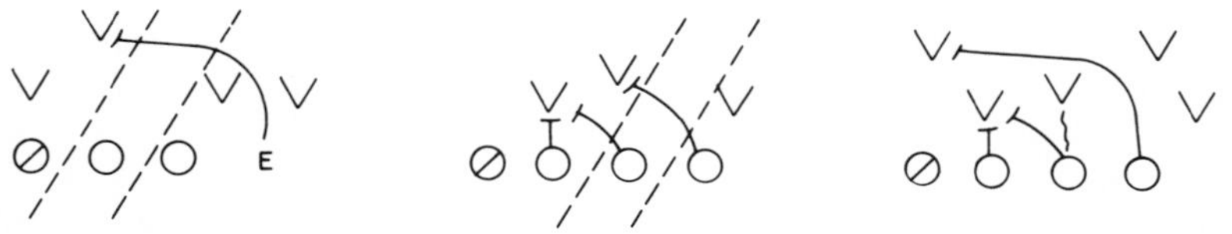

We usually keep the frontside end in tight which complements this trap. However, the end can do his job very adequately from a slot set if he is only flexed out from four to six feet.

Diagram 82: Frontside end play—3 trap (flexed end)

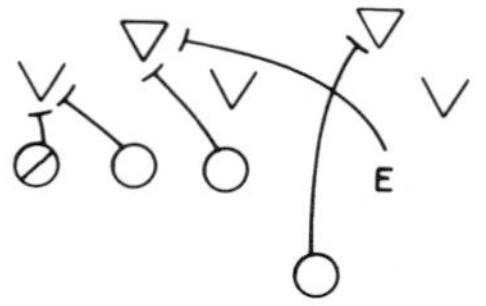

If we desire to split our end way out on the frontside, the play can still be run just as effectively by simply exchanging the assignments of the end and flanker back.

This set sometimes clears the running lane much better than any other formation depending on how the opponent covers our split end.

Diagram 83: Frontside end play—3 trap (end and flanker change blocks)

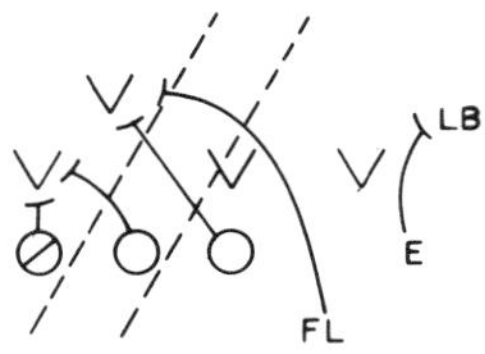

There are some games in which it might be desirable to arbitrarily switch the end's assignment to "outside linebacker" depending on the opponents' strengths and secondary sets. This is very easy to do, but the end must have practice on the change before he is asked to perform it in the game.

Diagram 84: Frontside end play—3 trap (LB outside special)

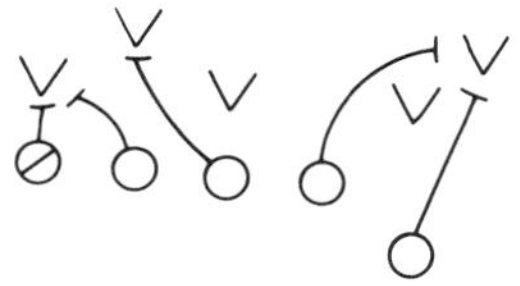

If our scout report tells us the outside linebacker is really tough, we make this adjustment. We like to two-time their best linebacker whenever possible. The end does block the outside linebacker when the play is a counter trap at 3.

We do prefer that the end blocks down to his inside, however, for his basic rule because we can then count on a two-time on the inside of the running lane against all standard defenses. *The inside seal on a trap is most important.* Any defender breaking through will surprise the runner from his blind side and can cause a fumble.

FRONTSIDE TACKLE PLAY—3 TRAP (INSIDE—LB INSIDE)

Inside rule

The tackle has a power block if there is a man on his inside. The guard is a post man unless there is a defensive man on his inside also. If he is posting he gives a word call such as "peaches" at the line of scrimmage indicating he will post. The tackle answers "cream" as a recognition signal.

To execute a power block, the tackle steps with his inside foot first closing the gap. He then sticks his helmet into the side of the

defender and drives him back. This post and power on the defensive guard seals the inside of the running lane very well.
Diagram 85: Frontside tackle—3 trap (inside rule)

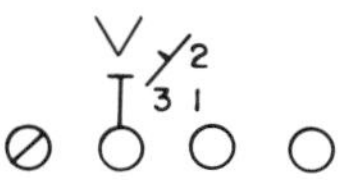

If the guard also has to block inside, he will say "no" at the line of scrimmage and the tackle executes a smear block taking the defender on his inside alone.
Diagram 86: Frontside tackle—3 trap (inside rule)

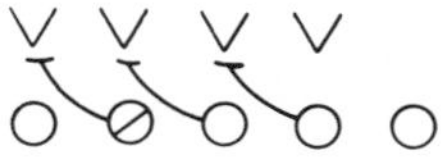

The tackle must still stop defensive penetration. Smear blocking means he will drive his head across the front of the defender by reaching with his outside arm for the charger's inside knee. He still steps to his inside as on the power block, but he must come down the line at a sharper angle. We drill on aiming for where the defender is going to be, not where he lines up.

LB inside rule

If there is no man inside, the tackle blocks the linebacker inside. An inside linebacker is any man from his outside shoulder into the center that is standing up. He still steps with his inside foot first to keep the gap closed. In blocking the linebacker, he must drive straight into him keeping his balance. *He is not to leave his feet.* His helmet is aimed at the numbers. He uses short choppy steps at contact. The end will also be hitting the linebacker so there will be a two time sealing the inside of the running lane.
Diagram 87: Frontside tackle—3 trap (LB inside)

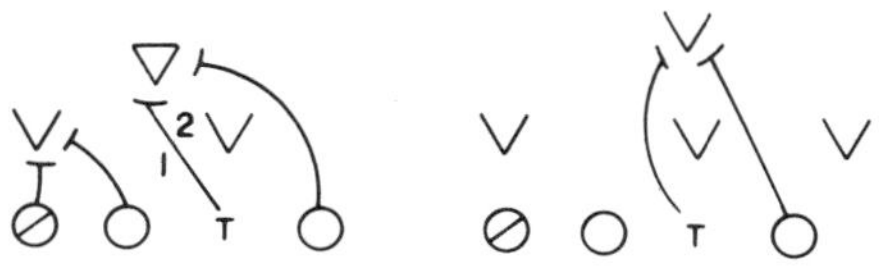

FRONTSIDE GUARD PLAY—3 TRAP (INSIDE-ON)

The guard's rule "inside-on" refers only to men on the line of scrimmage.

Inside

He checks to his inside first. If there is a man on the center, he will block him. As described in the tackle play, the guard becomes a power blocker when blocking a man the center is posting. The center signals the guard with a word call at the line of scrimmage telling him he will post. As with all power blocks, the guard steps with his inside foot first to seal the inside seam. He fires his head into the side of the defender and assists in driving him backwards using short choppy steps and working up on the defender.

Diagram 88: Frontside guard play—3 trap (inside rule)

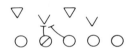

When the center is unable to post a man on his head because he must cover a backside defender, he tells the guard "no." The guard still blocks down on the man on his inside, but he now has to block the man alone. He uses a smear technique placing his head across the front of the defender to stop penetration. He steps with his inside foot first, but he goes down the line at a sharper angle than when posting.

Diagram 89: Frontside guard play—3 trap (inside rule)

On rule

If there is no man on his inside, he posts the man on him using a regular right shoulder block. His head is aimed at the belt, then he slides it to the left as the power blocker hits. He uses a word call to double check with the tackle that he is posting for him.

Diagram 90: Frontside guard play—3 trap (on rule)

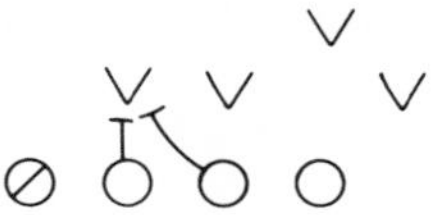

CENTER PLAY—3 TRAP (BACKSIDE-ON-OVER)

Backside rule

The center's first job is to cover for the pulling guard if there is a man "on" this guard. The puller gives a word call to the center to remind him to cover. The center blocks this man by himself. To stop penetration he uses a smear technique. On all cut-off blocks the center is taught to get his far side arm across in front of the charger. His first step is with the foot to the side he is going.

Diagram 91: Center play—3 trap (backside block)

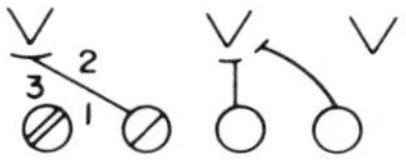

Crashing linebackers are played as "backside." If the scout report indicates a possible red-dog or if a coach sees a red-dog set up, the center is instructed to play them as "backside." In such cases the center signals the frontside guard that the post and power is off.

Diagram 92: Center play—3 trap (backside rule)

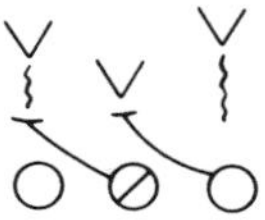

On rule

If no "backside," the center blocks "on." This means he is posting for the frontside guard. A post is executed with a near foot, near shoulder block leading with the foot on the power blocker's side. His head slides to the side opposite the power man. He signals the guard that he is posting for him with a word key.

Diagram 93: Center play—3 trap (on rule)

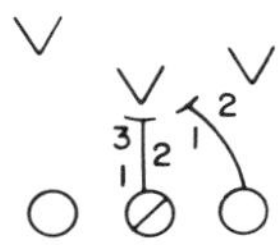

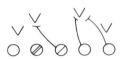

Over rule

The center takes the first linebacker away from the play if no "backside" or "on."

Diagram 94: Center play—3 trap (over rule)

BACKSIDE GUARD PLAY—3 TRAP (TRAP-IN)

The trapper's alignment enables him to step and pull without any delay because of the center's steps. His first step is a jab step with his lead foot in the direction he is pulling. He will get a good stride on the first step if his weight is on his outside foot. By pumping his arms and snapping his head and shoulders he can get the desired sixty-degree turn. He is *not* to pull back off the line of scrimmage.

Diagram 95: Backside guard play—3 trap (step and turn)

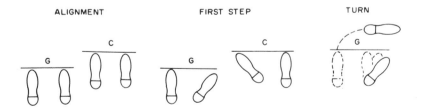

ALIGNMENT   FIRST STEP   TURN

His second step is along the line but up tight to the center and guard. He should keep his inside arm in contact with the blockers on his inside. He blocks any defender that comes to his face. He is to run a path up into the line anticipating a reaction to the inside by the defensive tackle. He must be prepared to go in after a defender and root him out. He is to contact the defensive man with his head on the inside. The further the defender crosses the line, the easier the block.

Diagram 96: Backside guard play—3 trap (trap-in)

ROOT HIM OUT   EASY PICK

The "pop" is extremely important on contact. The trapper needs to have a wide base with his knees flexed and his feet under him to really "pop."

If the defender doesn't charge, it poses no real problem. The puller has the inside-out block plus a running start. If the back runs close to the two-time block on the inside of the trap, there will be plenty of room.

Diagram 97: Backside guard—3 trap (no defensive charge)

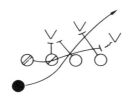

If the defender has reacted to the trap and has covered low to his inside, the trapper must smother him and seal him in by covering him with his body. The back cuts off the puller's butt and runs for daylight.

Diagram 98: Backside guard—3 trap (smother a low inside charger)

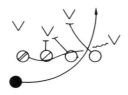

BACKSIDE TACKLE PLAY—3 TRAP (LANE RULE)

The tackle drop steps with his inside foot and pulls to the inside. This is an insurance move to prevent any defender from slashing through on the backside of the running lane. The reach technique is best to stop any penetrating chargers. If the center is slow and only gets a piece of his man on the backside, the tackle will pick him up, thereby preventing a backside collapse on the play.

Diagram 99: Backside tackle play—3 trap

BLOCKS RED-DOG   BLOCKS HARD CHARGER THAT CENTER MISSES

If the tackle reaches through, he will not only cut off the penetration, but many times he will keep his feet and continue on down field.

BACKSIDE END PLAY—3 TRAP (LANE RULE)

The end uses the same pulling technique to the inside if he is in a tight formation. He drop steps and reaches across in front of the defensive tackle.

Diagram 100: Backside end play—3 trap (lane rule)

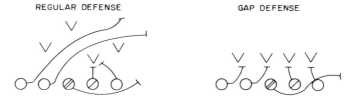

REGULAR DEFENSE   GAP DEFENSE

By making this a regular maneuver, no changes in procedure are needed when running the trap against a gap defense or as a counter play.

If the end is split, he just releases down field.

SUMMARY

When running the 3 trap, the frontside end should be a strong dependable blocker. He cracks down on the inside clearing the running lane from the outside in. The frontside tackle has to block either the inside defender or the inside linebacker. When blocking inside, he may have the opportunity to power block or he may have to smear block, thereby taking the inside man alone. The frontside guard posts the man "on" or blocks inside. When blocking inside, he may power or smear depending on the center's block.

The center protects his backside first. He uses the smear technique on all backside blocks whether it is a lineman or linebacker. When posting, the center uses a near foot near shoulder block. If the center has no man backside or on, he blocks the backside linebacker.

The pulling guard must stay up and in the line if he is to meet the defender with his head on the inside. The backside tackle and end help seal the backside by pulling to their right two steps before turning up field. They are to reach across the first defender to their inside and run.

9

TEACHING PLAY VARIETY WITH THE LONG TRAP

FLOW TRAP PLAYS

As with the short trap, a variety of plays may be run at this hole once the line becomes proficient in the blocking procedure. We run a tackle trap in each series regardless of formation or quarterback movement.

Both flow traps and counter traps may be run at the 3 hole. Because the tackle trap is wider than the short trap, it takes more time to break, and therefore, more flow is established. This means flow traps are quite effective.

The defensive flow is easily established by using sweeps or off tackle power plays. With both, the quarterback usually reverse pivots and either pitches or hands the ball to the trailback. If we are in the "T" formation, the trap play in the series would be called "left half at 3 trap."

The quarterback reverse pivots and hands the ball to the left half. The left half runs a path at the off tackle hole then cuts up. After being powered in a few times, the tackle is easy prey for the trapper because the backs all start for the tackle hole.

Diagram 101: Left half at 3 trap (power series)

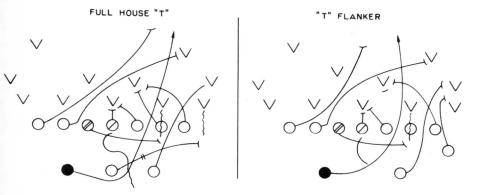

The play serves the same purpose when combined with the "I" power play.

Diagram 102: "I" left, left half at 3 trap (power series)

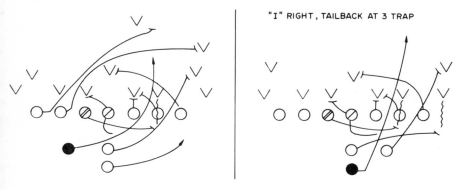

The first back at the hole blocks the linebacker. The second back blocks the end.

This trap may also be run with the fullback carrying the ball. This is usually executed as part of the belly series. The quarterback opens up and steps down the line as if to make a dive fake to the right half. He then turns back handing off to the fullback who delays and cuts up behind the quarterback.

We have the fullback use a cross-over step on this play. He plants his right foot on his second step and cuts up. The left half runs a wide pattern.

Diagram 103: Fullback at 3 trap

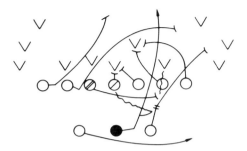

The 3 trap seems to be most effective when used as part of the quick pitch series. After pitching right to the right half or left to the left half with a flanker blocking on the corner, the trap is sprung. The quarterback reverse pivots and fakes a quick pitch to the right half. He slides down the line with a shuffle step as he follows through on the quicky fake. He then turns back giving the left half an inside handoff. The flanker blocks out on the outside linebacker while the right half turns up field to block the halfback. The left half steps to his right at the snap with his right foot. He cuts up on the third step by pushing off his right foot.

Diagram 104: Left half at 3 trap (quicky series)

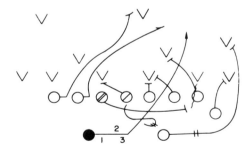

These traps hit with average quickness. If we have a really quick back and wish to rely on speed rather than the power of the blocking line, we call L.H. at 3 fast trap. On this play the quarterback reverses out to the flow and hands off immediately to the left half. The quarterback must get depth on his first two steps to clear himself from the running lane. The exchange with the half takes place on his second step.

The left half dives directly at the three hole stepping with his right foot first. He receives the ball on his second step. His right elbow is up. He cuts up into the hole by pushing off his right foot on his third step. He may be cheated up and to his right to increase the speed with which he hits the hole. The closer he is behind the puller the better.

Diagram 105: L.H. at 3 fast trap

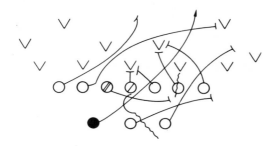

This play is generally more effective against odd defenses. The back's angle of entry at the hole helps the play to break better against a 5 man front.

The other backs fake a power play to the right.

COUNTERFLOW TRAPS

No major adjustments are needed in the line to run counterflow traps at the 3 hole. However, we do work with the right end on blocking a tough linebacker over him rather than having him block down on the center linebacker. The flow makes the block on the center linebacker fairly easy so that one man can handle him. At the same time the corner linebacker will be flowing in toward the center and will usually be in the end's area. We work on this option early in the season in drills so that it is a minor adjustment in game situations.

The backside tackle and end go through their regular assignment but we stress that they *must* drop step and cut off the first defender to their inside on counter traps.

The counter trap at the three hole is more delayed than the counter traps at 6 because the hole is slightly wider.

The halfback can counter at the three hole from any series or formation. The left half at three counter trap from the "T" belly series is especially good.

The quarterback reverse pivots faking to the fullback who hits up over the 6 hole. He helps to fill on the backside and is to block any defender in the area. Filling with the fullback is especially effective against odd defenses that are crashing linebackers.

The left half takes a short jab step with his left foot, plants it and cuts to his right just off the fullback's butt. We vary his alignment to gain the correct timing. Since this is an inside hand-off, his right elbow is up.

The quarterback continues his pivot, handing off with his right hand. He then continues on out to the left.

Diagram 106: Left half at 3 counter trap

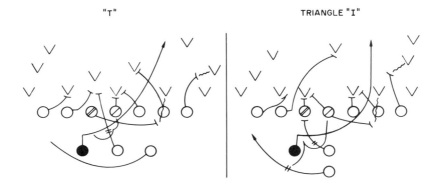

The crossing action of the fullback helps hide the countering left half.

The halfback counter from the dive has an entirely different look. The left half steps up toward the line with his left foot and cuts in the same manner.

The quarterback reverse pivots and gives the ball to the half on an inside hand off. Since the half doesn't have to wait for the fullback, he can cheat in and up a little.

The fullback runs his off tackle pattern while the right half goes wide around the end.

This counter trap develops quicker when run this way rather than having the quarterback come down the line forcing the left

Diagram 107: Left half at 3 dive counter trap

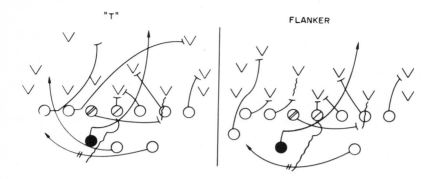

half to go around him. The half can cut up into the hole sooner because of the angle at the hole.

The same play may be executed without the reverse pivot if play system calls for it. He must come back deeper off the line if he opens to the half however, so that there is a direct running lane.

Diagram 108: Left half at 3 dive counter trap

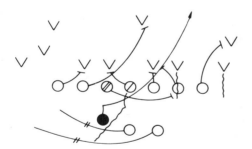

The fullback at 3 counter trap develops much quicker.

Diagram 109: Fullback at 3 counter trap ("T" formation)

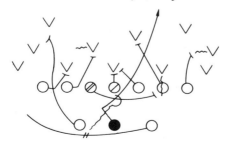

The left half follows his regular blocking path to the outside linebacker. The right half fakes an off tackle run. The fullback starts with a crossover step aiming his right toe at the guard's outside heel. On the second step, he plants his left foot and pushes to his right. His right elbow is up because this is an inside handoff.

The quarterback makes a short fake at the left half after his reverse pivot. He then hands off on his inside with his right hand. He should continue his fake on out to the left.

We allow the fullback to stay fairly erect on all counter traps. We want his weight under control so that he can slide for daylight.

This play fits into the "I" offense extremely well also.

Diagram 110: Fullback at 3 counter trap ("I" formation)

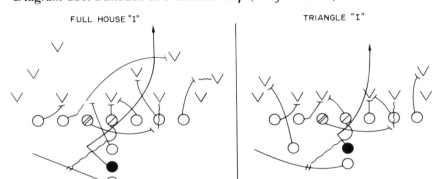

The frontside end is taught to block the outside linebacker on his side because he usually drifts into the running lane. This change is worked on in practice.

Diagram 111: Flanker at 3 trap

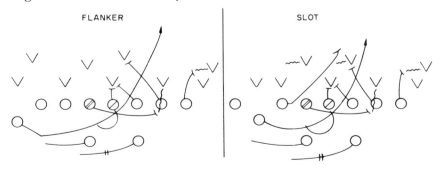

The wing reverse is another counterflow play that can be run at the 3 trap hole. The wing man is on the left. The quarterback reverses out and fakes the pitch to the right half. He then hands the ball off on an inside handoff to the wing man. By running the reverse out of the slot, the distance the wing has to run is cut down, thereby, speeding up the play.

The left half can dive to insure a backside seal but it isn't usually necessary. The adjustments are made in the line to pick up a crashing linebacker. This is described under center play.

DRAW PLAYS WITH THE 3 TRAP

Draw plays are very effective when run off the 3 trap hole. The fullback or left half can carry the ball off drop back action.

Diagram 112: Left half at 3 trap draw

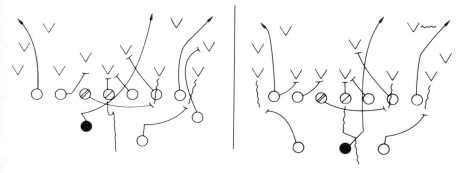

We like to use the left half for the draw off the 3 trap. The quarterback steps straight back holding the ball chest high and looking at the left end. The left half fakes a pass protection block, then comes across to his right taking an inside handoff. In this action the left half runs his path and the quarterback is responsible for getting him the ball when he breaks.

If sprint-out action is used, the left half stays on his spot faking a pass block while the quarterback runs to him.

The left half should cheat a little deeper for this play on alignment. We make a couple small adjustments for a draw trap. One is to have the tackle step to his inside and show a pass block before releasing. The second is that the ends run a down and out pattern to draw the secondary back from the action.

Diagram 113: Left half at 3 trap

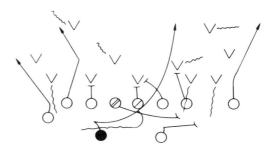

SUMMARY

Long Trap Plays

As with the short trap, it is necessary to teach the off-tackle trap rule for one hole only. It is not necessary that a team runs the play to both sides. By varying the sets and backfield maneuvers, all backs may carry the ball on a variety of plays through the same trap hole.

The key blockers in this play are the right end and tackle. In choosing personnel, the coach should seek a hard blocking right end if he expects to make the 3 trap an effective play.

The backs are taught to run close to the inside of the hole near the angle block or the post and power blocks. These blocks are more predictable than the trapper's block. The runner should square his shoulders to the line of scrimmage as he hits the hole.

The backside tackle and end must drop step and close down to stop penetration from the defense, especially on counter traps at the 3 hole.

If a team has exceptional pursuit, the flow traps work very well. If they like to red-dog, the draw traps probably will work better. An off-tackle trap is not as effective as a short trap vs. a red-dog defense because it takes more time to develop.

If the defensive pursuit is stopping the offense, counter traps off tackle will slow down their lateral movement.

10

SUCCESSFULLY TRAPPING WITH THE TACKLE

PULLING THE TACKLE

As the season progresses, teams begin to set defenses to key the guards of trapping teams. We then often trap with our tackle to keep the effectiveness in our trapping game. Many teams pull their tackles on traps as a basic trapping method. Personnel dictates a team's ability to do either or both.

If a team's tackles are too large or don't have the quick feet to pull, a coach should not waste the time teaching this play. But if either or both tackles are capable of trapping, it is an easy matter to adjust the rule for the long or short trap to accommodate the play because practically no change is needed. The guard merely exchanges assignments with the tackle.

Short Trap

Short trap rule (pulling the tackle)

FSE—over—LB outside—lane
FST—LB inside—outside
FSG—inside—outside
C—backside—on

BSG—backside—LB backside
BST—trap in
BSE—lane

Diagram 114 shows this 6 trap variation against a few standard defenses.

Diagram 114: 6 trap rule variation (pulling tackle)

5-4 DEFENSE

6-2 DEFENSE

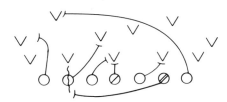
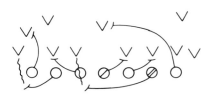

6-3 DEFENSE

4-4 DEFENSE

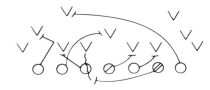
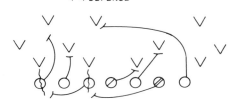

7 DIAMOND

4-4 NOTRE DAME

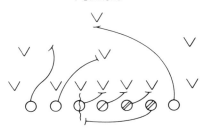
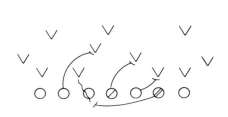

This combination is especially effective against the Notre Dame 4-4 because there are angles on every defender.

There is no change on the frontside blocking assignments. The center has his regular trap rule too, and he still covers for the guard as always. The backside guard blocks out rather than pulling. He steps with his outside foot first, hitting with his head on the inside of the defender. He blocks the defender playing on or over the tackle.

The backside tackle pulls down the line taking a short jab step with his inside foot. He must stay low and up in the line. He blocks the first defender past the center that shows in his face.

Even though the rule adjustment is simple, drill on the tackle's pull is necessary.

Play Variety

Because trapping with the tackle slows the development of the play, we usually run backfield maneuvers that take a little more time to break such as the wing reverse, right half at 6 counter trap or a draw trap.

Wing Reverse

Many teams combine their reverse from the wing with the pulling tackle for a trap reverse play. One advantage in pulling the tackle over pulling the guard is that the wing does not have to cheat in or start in motion to hit the hole as it breaks. Another is that if a team pulls their guards on all traps except the wing reverse, the defensive keys will have a great deal of trouble reading the play.

Diagram 115: Wing reverse at 6 trap (tackle pull)

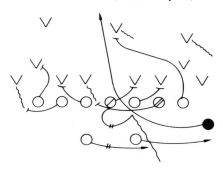

In executing the play the quarterback reverses out and fakes a pitch to the half. He then hands the ball off on his inside to the wing man. The timing may be worked out by adjusting the alignment of individual backs, however the play can be run well by starting all backs at the snap.

Halfback counter trap

The right half at 6 counter trap may be run with the tackle doing the trapping.

Diagram 116: Right half at 6 counter trap (tackle pull)

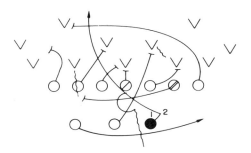

The fullback steps to his right with his right foot first turning his shoulders slightly to the right. This motion gives the tackle time to clear. The fullback then pushes off the right foot and cuts up over the guard's area and blocks sealing the backside of the play.

The right half takes a short step with the left foot, plants his right foot and cuts. He follows the tackle down the line looking for daylight on his inside. The play should be timed so that the half breaks immediately behind the fullback.

Draw trap

Another trap that has enough natural delay to be run with the tackle pulling is the draw. The half breaks off the tackle's rear with almost perfect timing when the draw is run off the sprint-out action.

The quarterback reverses out and sprints to a spot directly behind the right half carrying the ball in both hands at chest height. Just before he reaches the half he says "go." The half then forms a pocket and turns taking one step toward the hole. The half keeps the tackle in view at all times so as to judge where the hole will be. When he receives the ball, he cuts for daylight. The depth of the half should be adjusted according to the tackle's speed.

Diagram 117: Right half at 6 draw trap

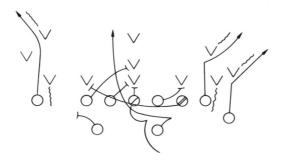

Long Trap

Pulling the tackle on the long trap slows the plays down considerably. Some teams use this maneuver for their long reverse or when they have a double fake in the backfield. The rule needs very little adjustment to pull the tackle. In our numbering system this is still called the 3 trap.

Long trap rule (pulling the tackle)

FSE—over—LB inside
FST—inside—inside linebacker
FSG—inside-on
  C—backside-on-over
BSG—backside-backside LB
BST—trap in
BSE—lane

Below are a few diagrams of the 3 trap rule against basic defenses.

Diagram 118: 3 trap rule (tackle pull)

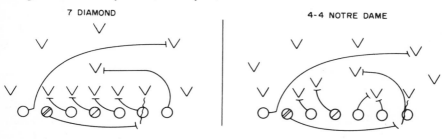

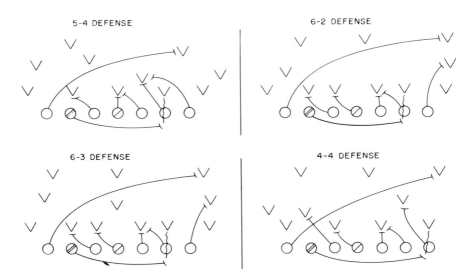

The major adjustments are that the backside end does not have to close down the line and seal because the guard is blocking out on the backside. The tackle has been sealing the backside by using a pulling motion so the technique is not new to him.

The frontside end must adjust on all counters and block the over man when he is in the end's immediate area. Over is written into his rule to remind him of this.

Diagram 119: Frontside end play (3 trap pulling the tackle)

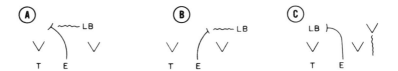

Play Variety

The left half at 3 counter trap is a good delay play to run in combination with the pulling tackle.

The quarterback reverses out, fakes a pitch to the right half, levels off and hands the ball to the left half with an inside handoff.

The left half steps with his left foot, plants and cuts. He follows right behind the tackle. With the fullback flankered, the half can

Diagram 120: Left half at 3 counter trap

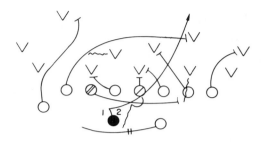

cheat up close behind the tackle to help hide his counter motion.

This play may also be run with the fullback in the "T." This play is extremely popular with the teams using the wishbone "T."

Diagram 121: Left half at 3 counter trap

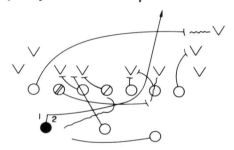

The correct timing is not difficult to achieve for this counter because of the wide split in the backfield and the closeness of the fullback.

The quarterback reverses out allowing the fullback to pass. He hands the ball to the left half with an inside handoff.

The left half jab steps with his left foot and cuts. As he hits the hole he must square his shoulders and turn up field. The fullback steps laterally with his left foot first to allow the pulling tackle to pass. He then fakes taking a handoff as he passes the quarterback. He fill blocks the backside with the center.

Wing Reverse

The wing reverse is a play that is commonly run with the tackle pulling instead of the guard. The play may be run from a flanker or slot formation, thereby allowing the coach to use either a half or fullback on the wing to carry the ball.

Diagram 122: Flanker at 3 trap

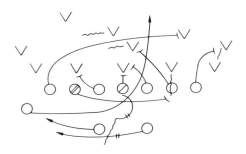

The quarterback reverses out, fakes a pitch to the right half, and hands the ball off on an inside handoff to the flanker. The flanker should get depth on his first steps so that he is angling in toward the hole at the exchange point. His shoulders should be turned in as he receives the ball. The quarterback watches the flanker from the moment he turns out.

If the linebackers are shooting on and off, the fullback can be used to seal the backside by faking him into the 6 hole first. This crossing motion helps to hide the reverse motion of the wing man. The quarterback should still make his fake to the right half, however. He needs depth to clear the running lane for the wing man. If he stays in and fakes a dive to the fullback, the smoothness of the play is hampered.

Diagram 123: Flanker at 3 trap—fullback dive

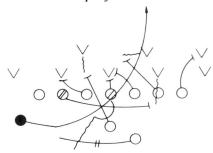

Draw trap

The left half at 3 draw trap with sprint-out action may be run very effectively with the tackle trapping.

Diagram 124: Left half at 3 draw trap—sprint-out

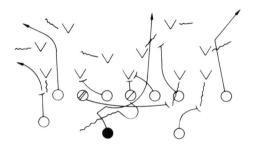

The draw off sprint-out action is slightly different from drop back action. The left half holds his pass block until the quarterback says "go." The quarterback turns and sprints toward the half holding the ball at chest height. His eyes are fixed on the left end. When he hands off the ball he must look at the half, *not* at the end.

The left half cheats deeper and wider on this play. The ends run out patterns. The flanker can hit the defensive end for two counts before running his out pattern in order to slow the rush. If the line is split, it is very doubtful that a defensive end could cause any problem on the play, but he should still slow the end up.

SUMMARY

Adjusting the trap rule to pull the tackle on trap plays is an easy matter, but teaching the tackle to pull can be very difficult. Trapping with the tackle may relieve the pressure of the keys on pulling guards, but the play will develop slower.

The best play combinations for the trap when pulling the tackle are reverses and draws.

Many teams have had great success trapping with the tackle.

III

Trapping Stunting Defenses

When the defense is using interior stunts with loops, slants and red-dogs, the best offensive weapons are usually the sweep, short passes, or straight ahead quick hitters. However, these defenses may also be trapped effectively.

Stunting defenses shoot men to a predetermined point. They do not read and flow. The defensive personnel "sell out" on their charge with their weight well forward. A trapping offense can take advantage of this type of charge and actually turn the added force of the charge into a disadvantage for the defense.

By using the techniques and word calls already taught, the line will be able to block the correct men on any stunt that they recognize. The immediate problem in high school is recognition of the stunt. If the coaching staff has an efficient scouting program and films of their opponents, problems in recognizing defenses are reduced considerably.

If trap plays are a part of the game plan and are run against the opponents' defenses in practice, they will work in the game. Many times a trap is more effective against the stunt than a regular play because the blocker is taking advantage of the uncontrolled charge at the point of attack.

The quicker a play hits against a stunt, the less chance the blocking will break down. It is not a good idea to run delay plays or plays that require the quarterback to travel along the line of scrimmage with his fakes against stunting defenses. Therefore, in trapping these defenses the plays that are most successful are the ones that hit quickly, require very little footwork by the quarterback and approach the line of scrimmage straight on.

11

TRAPPING THE GAP EIGHT DEFENSE

The trap is an integral part of our goal line offense. Our game plan each week includes three or four basic goal line plays that the quarterback may call. One of these plays is always a trap.

Many teams hesitate to use traps on the goal line because of the low hard inside charge of the defense or because of the need to change their rules when facing gaping defenses. Actually the low sell out defensive charge is to the offense's advantage especially if the smear technique has been mastered. We have also found that our rules need little or no modification to trap gaping defenses.

Short Traps

The only change made when we are running the short trap against a gap defense is the frontside guard blocks to his outside rather than inside.

Diagram 125: 6 trap rule

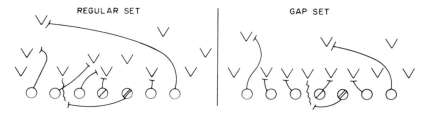

REGULAR SET   GAP SET

In executing either the short or long trap vs. the gap eight, all linemen must use the smear technique (head across the front, reverse shoulder, step with the near foot) because all defenders are divorced from them half a man. Since this has been taught as a part of the blocking system no new techniques are needed to trap low hard charging gap defenses.

It should also be noted that the backside tackles have been taught to drop step and close down hard on traps regardless of the defense, so no new techniques have to be taught on the backside.

Diagram 126: Right half at 6 counter trap vs. gap 8 defense

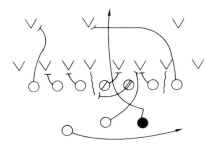

The short trap against the gap 8 actually becomes a cross block between the guard and center. All linemen have an angle except the backside tackle. He must drop step and close hard. To be sure the man over the tackle is blocked, we often run the scissors trap using the fullback as an extra blocker at the hole. In executing this play the quarterback reverse pivots, fakes to the fullback and hands to the right half. The fullback steps to his right leading with the right foot. He blocks the first defender to show in his path. The right half jab steps with his right foot first. He pushes off his right foot cutting behind the fullback. He takes the handoff with his left elbow up. As he breaks through the line, he looks to his right for the releasing end to cut off his block.

If the backside tackle can handle his man, the most effective short trap against the gap is a quick hitter with the fullback.

The right half blocks the first defender outside the tackle. The fullback steps to the right with his right foot first, plants it and cuts up immediately behind the pulling guard.

It should be reemphasized here that the pulling guard on the short trap uses more of a cross blocking technique than a pulling

Diagram 127: FB at 6 counter trap vs. gap 8

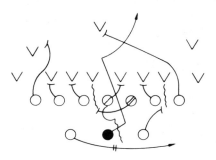

technique. His first move is to jab step with his left foot toward the center turning his shoulders at a 45° angle, not around to 90°. He continues up into the line with his second step on a 45° angle. After reaching this position he can turn out for his block. Moving up into the line close to the center will enable the trapper to meet the defender's low inside charge with his head on the inside.

The Long Trap

The long trap is an excellent play to use against gaping defenses. The only rule adjustment made is that the frontside tackle is taught to block *outside* rather than inside when trapping the gap 8.

Diagram 128: 3 trap rule

REGULAR SET   GAP SET

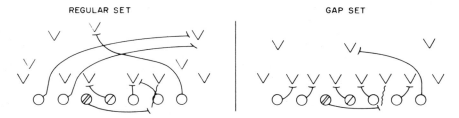

Making this minor adjustment in the blocking rules adds greatly to the effectiveness of long trap plays used against goal line defenses. It shortens the distance the trapper has to pull. It gives the interior defender less time to react to the trapper. It eliminates one defender that can break through an inside seam into the path of the ball carrier and it shortens the lateral distance the runner has to move in his running lane before cutting up field. The hole is too strung out if the tackle blocks in. This adjustment does not alter the backfield timing on the trap play.

The left half at 3 trap from a flanker or slot set is a strong play against a gap 8 defense.

Diagram 129: Left half at 3 trap—gap 8

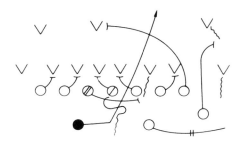

The gap 8 has a strong concentration of defenders in the middle but no depth in defenders. This defense is hard pressed to cover an attack at the corner. The slot set spreads the gap 8 defenders even thinner than normal and places an extra blocker, the slot man, in a good position to get a key block.

This play is very effective when run in combination with quick pitches and sprintouts from the flanker or slot formation.

The draw trap is another play that cracks the gap 8 extremely well. A team using this defense relies on its pass rush and short coverage. This means the interior defenders must be coming hard and deep in a pass situation making any one of them vulnerable to the trap. The secondary can lend no assistance for they must spread out and be prepared to cover three receivers immediately.

Both halves show a pass block. The left half sets up for one count, turns and loops into the trap hole squaring his shoulders at the handoff point. The quarterback retreats only a couple of steps straight back looking at the left end so as to see the left half's action.

He must place the ball in the left half's pocket when the half cuts.
Diagram 130: Left half at 3 draw trap—gap 8

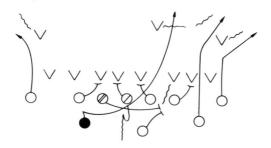

SUMMARY

The trap should be a part of the goal line offensive plan because it takes advantage of the hard defensive charge. Gaping defenses are easily trapped for long gains because they have no defenders in depth and they can be forced to spread their secondary to cover wide sets.

Every team should run their goal line offense at least three times a week for ten minutes or more vs. gap defenses. This practice procedure combined with line drill on blocking the trap against the gap eight will help insure satisfactory results when your team is inside the opponent's fifteen yard line or when facing a team that reverts to a gap 8 in short yardage situations.

12

TRAPPING RED-DOG DEFENSES

The most common interior stunts faced by teams are the center linebacker red-dogs. Most of these red-dogs are executed from odd fronts and place the bulk of their pressure on the center and guards. The crashing center linebacker from a 5-3 set is a good example of this stunt.

TRAPPING THE 5-3 STUNT

In the 5-3 defense the center linebacker usually coordinates his stunts with the nose guard. One man loops over a guard's head while the other slants in over the opposite guard.

Diagram 131: Center linebacker stunt

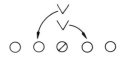

The short trap is effective against this stunt because it hits straight at it, right now.

The center's rule is "backside-on" so he blocks the man "on" riding him down the line and out of the play because his defensive charge is out of the hole.

111

Diagram 132: 6 trap versus linebacker stunt right

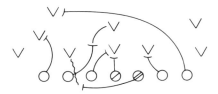

The left guard's rule is "inside-outside" so he fires to the inside area blocking the first man to show in his face. If the center linebacker slashes into him, he blocks him. If the linebacker is looping to the outside, the guard will not see him so he blocks the center guard.

Diagram 133: Left guard blocking on 6 trap-center stunt

The left tackle's rule is "inside linebacker." He blocks down inside picking up the center linebacker. If the offensive guard happens to contact the center linebacker, too, it just helps the tackle perform his block. However, if the linebacker is crashing into him, the tackle hits low with his head on the inside.

Diagram 134: Left tackle blocks—5-3 center stunt

When the center linebacker charges to his left and the nose man to the right, a slightly different pattern is presented, but the blocking rules automatically compensate.

The center is firing straight out to block his "on" man against odd defenses most of the time. If his "on" man charges toward the 6 hole from a stunt set, the center goes right on past him and picks up the charger going to the backside of the play because his rule is "backside-on." He must protect the backside first. This happens very quickly, but even if the center gets only a small piece of the linebacker, the play will go because the runner is cutting away from the stunt and many times other blockers are filling for the puller, too.

Diagram 135: Center's block—6 trap—linebacker stunt left

The left guard is blocking to his inside anticipating a hit on the nose man so his block is one-on-one. He has been taught to step inside first and aim his helmet for the rib cage so he will not miss the nose man whether he is posted by the center or not. The center can aid the guard by saying "no" if he recognizes the linebacker stunt at alignment. The left tackle seals inside starting for the center linebacker. Since his man stunted out of the play, he just walls inside picking up the first defender in his face. Many times he will hit the nose man sliding to the outside. He may have to go as deep as the safety for a block.

Diagram 136: Left tackle block—6 trap—linebacker stunt left

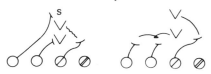

SHORT TRAP PLAY SELECTION AGAINST THE CENTER STUNT

One of the quickest hitting short traps to run against this stunt is the fullback at 6 counter trap (*Diagram 137*).

A 6 trap play that picks up center stunts regardless of the strength of the stunter is "I" fullback at 6 counter trap or "T" right half at 6 counter trap (*Diagram 138*).

The upback hits in over the pulling guard sealing the backside in case the center misreads the stunt or the linebacker is shooting on his own with the nose guard staying head up (*Diagram 139*).

The fullback hits in over the pulling guard, sealing the backside even if the center misreads the stunt.

Diagram 137: Fullback at 6 counter trap—center stunt

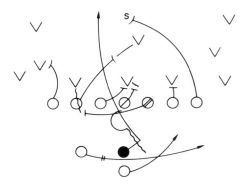

Diagram 138: "I" fullback at 6 counter trap

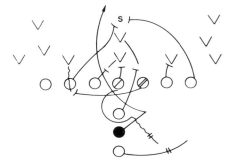

Diagram 139: "T" right half at 6 counter trap

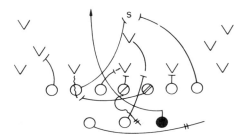

Poor selections of 6 trap plays against a center stunt would be right half at 6 trap and flanker at 6 trap.

Diagram 140: Right half at 6 trap

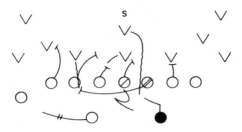

The right half is traveling across the danger area. If the center misses his block entirely, the half is likely to meet the linebacker head on.

The flanker at 6 counter trap is a delay counter to be used against reading defenses, *not* against stunting defenses. The center area will often collapse before the flanker passes the critical point if used when the red-dog is on.

Diagram 141: Flanker at 6 counter trap—center stunt

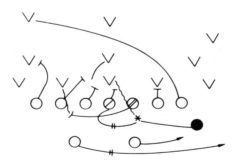

LONG TRAPS AGAINST THE CENTER STUNT

This stunt poses no real problems for the long trap. The techniques that are used for short trap also apply to the long trap against odd fronts. The long trap should hit to the opposite side of the line, however, so the play described here is the 3 trap.

Diagram 142: 3 trap– Linebacker stunt left

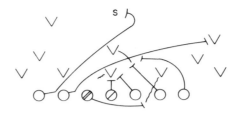

The center's rule is "backside-on" for all traps so he fires out at the man on his nose. If the nose man charges backside, the center blocks him on down the line. If his nose man stunts toward the hole and the center linebacker red-dogs to the backside, the center picks up the linebacker crashing to his backside. *The center must be backside conscious.*

Diagram 143: Center play 3 trap—linebacker stunts

The block required of the center is not difficult to teach, but he must work on his reaction in practice.

The frontside guard's rule is "inside-on," so he is blocking inside. He hits the first man coming into his face.

Diagram 144: Frontside guard—3 trap center stunt

The guard fires down tight to his inside stepping with his inside foot first anticipating a power block on the nose man. If the nose man comes, he sticks him driving his helmet into the rib cage. If the linebacker comes, there will be a collision; but the guard has help from the tackle who is sealing to his inside, also.

The frontside tackle's rule is "inside-linebacker inside." If the linebacker loops away, he just seals the inside blocking the first defender from the line of scrimmage to the safety area that comes his way. If the linebacker crashes to his side or stands, the tackle blocks him.

Diagram 145: Frontside tackle play—3 trap—center stunt

It should be pointed out that even though the three trap breaks a little slower against some defenses than the 6 trap, it is extremely effective in hitting the odd front. One reason is that there are additional blockers to pick up interior defenders. The backside tackle has a lane rule, but he is taught to drop step and pull inside before releasing. This means he is assisting the center by sealing the backside.

The frontside end also has a "linebacker inside" rule. He is looking for a two-time block with the tackle on the linebacker. This means that the center linebacker will normally be blocked by two men on the 3 trap no matter which way he shoots or drifts irregardless of the nose guard's charge.

Diagram 146: 3 trap—two time blocks on center linebacker

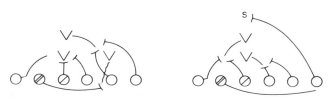

If the end meets no resistance on the inside, he turns up into the safety area and seals the running lane.

3 TRAP PLAY SELECTIONS VERSUS THE CENTER STUNT

One trap that gets into the three hole in a hurry is the fullback at 3 counter trap.

Diagram 147: Fullback at 3 counter trap—center stunt

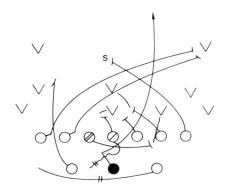

The faster the play hits, the less chance that the blocking will break down.

Other good play selections would be "T" left half at 3 counter trap or "I" fullback at 3 counter trap.

Diagram 148: Left half 3 counter trap—center stunt

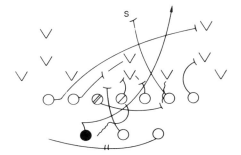

Since the fullback seals the "backside," it doesn't matter if the center reads the stunt or not. When a back is filling for a pulling guard, he should tell the center in the huddle so that the center can block straight on paying no attention to stunts. We do not tell the center this is possible until after we have taught him to block the center stunt. Some offenses key the blocking so that a word call such as "counter" tells the center that he does not have to block "backside" on a trap.

Here the upback is shown filling the backside as the center blocks on the nose guard. The backside tackle blocks in the line on

Diagram 149: "I" fullback at 3 counter trap—center stunt

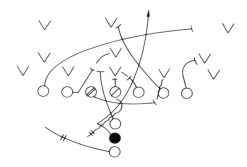

this stunt only when he contacts a defender in his release lane. If the linebacker's stunt is wide, he will be picked up by this block.

SUMMARY

**Short and Long Traps
versus Center Stunt**

The 3 or 6 trap is an effective play versus the center stunt. The center must work on picking up the charger to the backside of the play. To help the center in case he is unaware of the stunt, the counter traps should be so formulated that the fullback or upback is filling for the pulling guard.

The quicker the trap hits, the less chance the blocking will break down from the force of the red-dog. Do *not* run slow reverse traps against red-dog defenses.

TRAPPING THE 5-4 RED-DOG WITH THE SHORT TRAPS

Even though the defense can stunt with two center linebackers from the 5-4, the defensive stunts are not hard to block.

If a team blows the linebackers straight in throughout the game, the center tells the guards he will block the linebacker as "backside" on traps. This means the frontside guard blocks the nose man by himself using a smear technique (head across the front). The center may make the call at the line scrimmage or in the huddle. If the linebackers step up close when they are red-dogging, he can call the post and power off at the line.

The center tells the guard "no." The guard then realizes the "post" is off so he must smear block on the nose man.

The frontside tackle has a tough block. He must close his split and fire down the line to his inside for a spot behind the heels of the

Diagram 150: Center-guard blocking—6 trap versus 5-4 red-dog

center in order to get his head across the front of the crasher.
Diagram 151: Tackle block—6 trap—5-4 red-dog

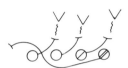

BLOCKING ADJUSTMENT NO. 1—6 TRAP—RED-DOGGING LINEBACKERS

If the crashing linebacker is breaking through the tackle's block on the 6 trap, the simplest adjustment is to let the linebacker come in and trap him instead of the tackle.

The center still blocks the backside crasher as "backside." The guard blocks inside on the nose man, but the tackle blocks the man on his nose letting the linebacker come in. The trapper is taught to block out on the first man past the center anyway so trapping the linebacker is not a change for him. In fact, a hard charging linebacker is often an easier block for the trapper than a lineman. He can use the charger's momentum to carry him further from the play.
Diagram 152: Fullback at 6 counter trap—5-4 red-dog—trapping the linebacker

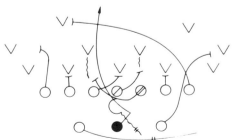

This play hits the hole quickly and keeps the runner out of the red-dogger's line of fire. However, the ball carrier must concentrate on cutting off the back of the trapper as the guard passes the center. Then he starts his slide to his left. In running close to the angle block of the down linemen, there is less chance that the linebacker will get an arm on him.

BLOCKING ADJUSTMENT NO. 2—6 TRAP—RED-DOGGING LINEBACKERS

If the linebacker over the 6 hole is too strong or too quick for the tackle, the line can double team him on some 6 trap plays by making a blocking rule adjustment for the guard. The center is told to block his regular 6 trap rule "backside-on" which means he hits the man on his nose. He will be blocking him alone, however. The frontside tackle blocks his regular trap rule "inside linebacker." The frontside guard is told to block the crashing linebacker. The lead back fills for the pulling guard by blocking the backside crashing linebacker.

Diagram 153: "T" right half at 6 counter trap—5-4 red-dog double team the linebacker

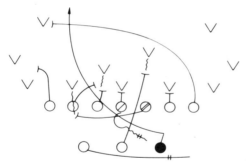

Diagram 154: "I" fullback at 6 counter trap—5-4 red-dog double team the linebacker

TRAPPING THE 5-4 RED-DOG WITH THE LONG TRAP

The long trap may also be run against the 5-4 red-dog defense. Remember the long and short trap rules work out to use almost the same blocking procedures against an odd defense. The 3 trap blocking assignments for the center and frontside guard and tackle are the same as the assignments were for the frontside on the 6 trap.

To apply the 3 trap rule against a 5-4 red-dog, the center is taught to block the crashing linebacker as if he were "backside." He must then signal the frontside guard to block the nose man alone. The guard will then use a smear technique (head in front) in attacking the middle guard so as to stop penetration. The frontside tackle blocks the center linebacker alone.

Diagram 155: 3 trap blocking versus 5-4 red-dog

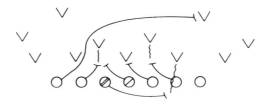

The backside tackle and end pull down the line and wall up the inside seams as the backside guard pulls to execute the trap. This drop step and pull by the backside tackle helps the center in sealing the backside. Often the tackle and center meet head on forcing the red-dogger to the outside. Because the backside is sealed, a greater variety of trap plays may be run. For example, left half at 3 trap is a safe play even though the linebacker is coming hard.

Diagram 156: Left half at 3 trap—5-4 red-dog

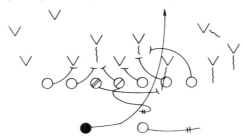

The left half is deep enough to run a path behind the pulling guard and not receive interference from the backside defenders when the center and guard are closing the seam.

The fullback at 3 counter trap is a quicker hitting play plus its movement will draw the red-doggers to the left as the fullback breaks to the right.

Diagram 157: Fullback at 3 counter trap—5-4 red-dog

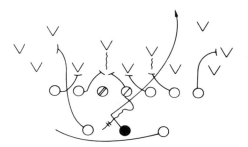

BLOCKING ADJUSTMENT NO. 1—3 TRAP—RED-DOGGING LINEBACKERS

When the frontside linebacker is crashing so hard that the frontside tackle can't handle him, the easiest adjustment is to trap the linebacker as he comes in.

Diagram 158: 3 trap—5-4 red-dog—trapping the linebacker

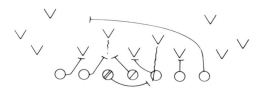

This adjustment is easy to teach because the center and frontside guard block their regular 3 trap rule. The frontside tackle is told to block "on" rather than "inside linebacker."

Again it should be emphasized that the backs must run for daylight. The hole is usually closer to the center when the linebacker is trapped.

BLOCKING ADJUSTMENT NO. 2—3 TRAP—
RED-DOGGING LINEBACKERS

If the nose man is too quick to be blocked by the guard because of the angle, the center can post if a back is used to fill for the pulling guard. A play such as left half at 3 counter trap is a good example of this change.

Diagram 159: Left half at 3 counter trap—5-4 red-dog—posting the nose man

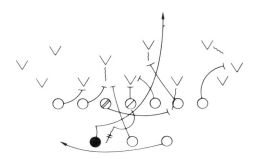

SUMMARY

Short and Long Traps versus 5-4 Red-Dog Defenses

The 3 and 6 trap may be run against the 5-4 red-dog by simply having the center block a crashing linebacker as if he were "backside." However, the nose man may still be two-timed if the fullback is used to cover for the pulling guard. Lastly, if the frontside red-dogger is coming in too hard to be blocked by the tackle, he may be defeated by letting him rush across the line and then trapping him.

13

TRAPPING TANDEM SETS

Many times the defense will place red-dogging linebackers in tandem behind down linemen. From this alignment they may stunt in any direction which can be very confusing to high school blockers. The blocking techniques a team uses when faced with this defense must be thoroughly understood by the line and drilled on if any success is to be achieved. One good method of attacking tandem sets is to trap them. Of course, some traps will be more successful than others depending on where the defense places their tandem charges.

THE SHORT TRAP VERSUS TANDEM SETS OVER THE GUARDS

Teams using even defenses such as a 4-4 or 6-2 wide tackle often place their tandem sets over the guards.

Diagram 160: 4-4 tandem stunt

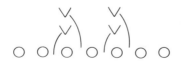

Normally the short trap should not be a part of the game plan when facing a team using this set as a basic defense. There are too many defenders crashing in a small area to have consistent success. Another problem is that the trapper has to go the same distance to get to the block as the stunting defender does to get to his assigned spot. The 6 trap rule will open holes against this set, however.

Diagram 161: 6 trap—tandem set over guards

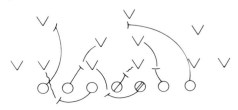

No special adjustments are needed to enable the line to pick up every defender. They must be conscious of blocking an area, however. The center blocks "backside" taking the first man to charge into his face. The backside tackle steps to his inside closing the seam and blocks the man charging into his shoulder.

Diagram 162: 6 trap—tandem set—center and backside tackle blocks

It should be noted that both blockers shoot their head across the front of the defender in an effort to close the seam and stop penetration.

The pulling guard traps the first man past the center that crosses his face. He must be stepping up and in with his face up. The frontside tackle fires down inside anticipating a block on the linebacker. If the linebacker stunts inside, he will be trapped. If he stunts outside, the tackle will hit him.

Diagram 163: 6 trap tandem stunt—pulling guard and frontside tackle blocks

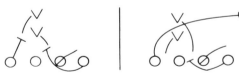

The tackle continues on across the hole and blocks through the running lane if the linebacker has shot away from him.

The defensive guard is trapped if he comes inside. If he goes outside, he generally takes himself out of the play. However, the fullback can pick him up if the 6 trap is run out of a "T."

Diagram 164: "T" right half at 6 trap—tandem stunt

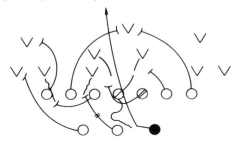

If the defense is reading and flowing with this set, the best 6 traps would be counters with the right half or flanker.

Diagram 165: Right half at 6 counter trap—tandem flowing

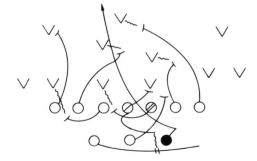

Diagram 166: Flanker at 6 counter trap—tandem flowing

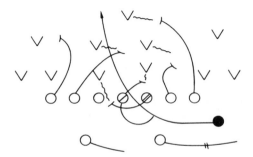

When the defense has a tendency to red-dog from this tandem set, the only safe 6 trap to place in the game plan would be a quick hitter such as the fullback at 6 counter trap.

Diagram 167: Fullback at 6 counter trap—tandem red-dog

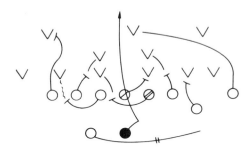

THE LONG TRAP VERSUS TANDEM SETS OVER THE GUARDS.

The three trap is often a good play to run against the tandem set over the guards because the inside is well sealed and no outside linebackers can drift into the play.

Diagram 168: 3 trap rule—tandem set

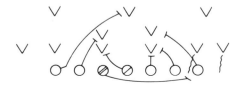

No special adjustments are made when trapping this set, however a few techniques are stressed in practice. The backside tackle must be sure to drop step and seal before he starts up field. He may have to pick up the guard stunting outside or the linebacker. The center in blocking backside picks up the man who charges into his face.

Diagram 169: 3 trap—tandem over guards center
and backside tackle blocks

The frontside guard, tackle and end all seal to their inside by stepping with their inside foot first. If the linebacker is stunting, the guard and tackle use the smear block (head across the front) hitting the man who charges into them.

Diagram 170: 3 trap—tandem set over guards frontside blocks

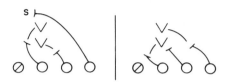

The guard charges at the defensive guard placing his head on the inside. If the linebacker comes, he fires on across at the linebacker with his head in front of the charge. The tackle steps down the line anticipating he may have to block the defensive lineman alone using a smear technique. If he gets the guards help, it will be a stronger block. The end comes down hard on the inside linebacker. If the linebacker has charged away from the play, he turns up field into the safety.

Since the blocking angles on the inside are so strong against this defensive set, the only long traps needed are the flow traps. One such play would be left half at 3 trap.

Diagram 171: Left half at 3 trap—tandem set

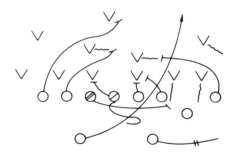

This play is very effective when run from a flanker or slot because the wider set spreads the defense and the pitch fake holds the wide defenders to the outside allowing the runner to cut in behind them.

SUMMARY

Trapping Tandem Sets over the Guards

The defenses that use a tendem set over the guards may be trapped. The long traps are more effective than short traps against this set. However, the short trap may be used if employed correctly. If the defense uses flowing linebackers, the best short trap is the counter. If the linebackers are red-dogging, the quick hitting short traps should be used.

THE SHORT TRAP VERSUS TANDEM SETS OVER THE TACKLES

Many teams use tandem sets over the tackles to discourage the off tackle power plays and to rush the passer. The short trap is especially effective against these defenses because the rule will block the sets with no adjustments.

Diagram 172: 6 trap v.s. tandem set over tackles

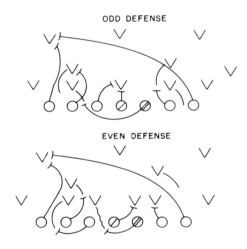

ODD DEFENSE

EVEN DEFENSE

The center blocks "on" if there is a man "on" and "backside" if no man is "on." The backside guard pulls up and in trapping the first man to come into his face. The backside tackle steps to his inside closing the seam. He blocks the defender charging inside. The backside end executes a shallow release.

The frontside guard blocks "inside" if there is a man on the center. If no man "inside," he blocks the first defender charging into his face on his outside. Against the tandem it may be either a linebacker or lineman, but usually he will hit the lineman no matter which way he charges.

The frontside tackle's rule is "inside linebacker—outside." The tandem linebacker, then, is his man. To be in position to screen him out of the play, he must step with his inside foot to the inside. If the linebacker stunts in, the tackle hits him with his head across the front. If the linebacker stunts out, he will be out of the play.

Diagram 173: Frontside guard and tackle play v.s. tandem set

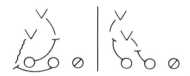

He may release inside the tackle if the tackle is playing head up, but if he is on the inside or charging inside, the offensive tackle must release around the defender.

Diagram 174: Frontside tackle releases for inside linebacker—tandem sets

The frontside end is blocking "over-outside linebacker—lane." In other words it is his job to cut off the first outside defender that can interfere with the runner.

The backside tackle closes his inside seam by stepping with his inside foot first and putting his head across the front of the charger who comes to the inside from the tandem set.

The backside end must release in a shallow path in order to block across the running lane before the runner breaks into the secondary.

The short trap will be much more effective against this set than against a tandem set over the guards. The red-dog on the outside does not jam the hole as tightly as the red-dog does when it is over the area being trapped. However, if the defense is red-dogging from this tandem set, the best 6 traps would be the ones that hit quickly such as right half at 6 quick trap.

Diagram 175: Right half at 6 quick trap

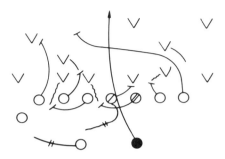

Quick trap means that the handoff is made before the fake, not after.

If the linebackers are flowing, counter traps should be used to draw them into their pursuit and then hit back against it. One such trap would be slot back at 6 counter trap.

Diagram 176: Slot back at 6 counter trap v.s. tandem set

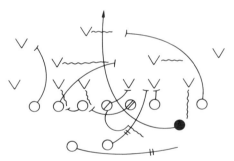

LONG TRAP V.S. TANDEM SETS OVER THE TACKLES

To make the long trap go against the wide tandem, two points must be stressed. The trapper must pull up and in so he doesn't pass a red-dogger and the back has to run tight to the "double-team" block.

The center has his regular 3 trap assignment "backside-on." The frontside guard has his regular assignment "on-inside." The backside tackle and end drop step and pull closing the inside seam. The puller stays up close to the two-time block. He blocks out on the first defender in his face keeping his head on the *inside*. The frontside tackle has to block "inside-inside linebacker." To get to his

Diagram 177: 3 trap—tandem set over tackles

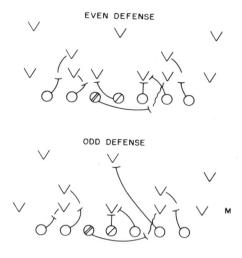

area he will have to release shallow to keep from being knocked off balance by the defender shooting his inside seam. If there is no inside man or linebacker, he proceeds up field and blocks across the running lane. The frontside end steps to his inside then up, looking for the inside linebacker. If the linebacker comes, he gets him. If he charges away, the end blocks on across the running lane.

Diagram 178: Frontside end play—3 trap—tandem set

The tackle is trapped on his inside charge. If the linebacker crashes inside, he will be trapped. The tackle's outside charge automatically takes him out of the play. Because the defenders are crashing into the running area, the runner must stay close to the inside of the running lane and rely on the two-time block.

Usually a wide set to the wide side of the field will influence the linebackers to crash outside. A good play to run against this set in this situation is left half at 3 trap from a slot or flanker formation because the runner is cutting in behind the defensive flow with a number of blockers sealing the inside of the running lane.

Diagram 179: Slot right, left half at 3 trap—tandem set over tackles

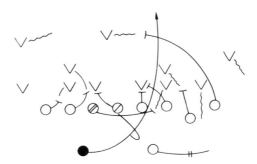

The wide set plus the outside fake tends to draw the defenders to the outside. The runner is to stay in tight, square his shoulders and cut up-field immediately.

Another play that breaks quickly against this set is fullback at 3 quick trap. The fullback is in a position to hit directly at the hole, therefore he can keep his shoulders square and look straight up the running lane.

Diagram 180: Wing right—fullback at 3 quick trap—tandem set over tackles

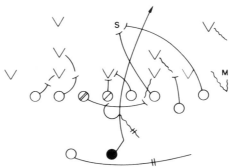

SUMMARY

One effective method of defeating red-dogging defenses in tandem sets is to trap them. The defender charging inside is trapped whether he is the lineman or linebacker. The offensive linemen must stop penetration along the line by smear blocking all crashing linebackers.

Quick hitting traps are used if the defense is red-dogging, but counters may be employed if the linebackers are flowing.

The short trap should be used sparingly against tandem sets over the guards. The long trap can be highly successful against this defense, however, because the inside of the running lane is sealed by three blockers and the backside linemen close their inside seams before releasing.

When the tandem is set wider over the tackle area, the short trap becomes a devastating weapon that can crack the defense for long gains. The long trap is still a good play to use against this set especially when run from wide spread sets in combination with sweeps and sprintout passes.

If the linebackers are breaking through on the backside, additional blocking strength can be gained by using the fullback to help cover for the pulling guard.

14

TRAPPING THE NOTRE DAME 4-4

If the trapping game is an insignificant part of a team's offense, they can block all defenses with the basic rule for the short or long trap with no adjustments. Of course, their trap plays will have only occasional success as would any other play in their offense including those using straight ahead blocking. When facing teams that use defenses that present unique problems, the coaching staff should review their plays and blocking procedures and formulate a game plan that will have some degree of predicted success and will instill confidence in the team. The correct choice of plays is certainly important in the game plan, but equally important is the adjustment of the blocking rules for the chosen plays. As with blocking the red-dogging linebackers and tandems we feel the trap becomes one hundred per cent more effective against the Notre Dame 4-4 when special adjustments are made in the rule or its interpretation to accommodate the peculiarities of the defensive set. In adapting the trap rules to block special sets, the coach must attempt to keep the changes to a minimum while eliminating the key problems and difficult techniques.

SHORT TRAPPING THE NOTRE DAME 4-4

As covered in earlier chapters, the short trap rule will block this 4-4. However, if a team uses the Notre Dame as its basic defense, they will play havoc with most of the interior trapping game unless adjustments are made. The regular 6 trap rule blocks this defense as follows.

Diagram 181: 6 trap rule regular—Notre Dame 4-4

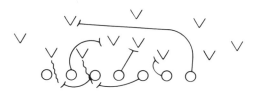

6 TRAP RULE REVIEW

FSE over—LB outside lane
FST LB inside—outside
FSG inside—outside
  C backside—on
BSG trap in
BST gap—on—over—outside
BSE lane

First back—LB outside

Even with no adjustments there are some unique situations presented here that must be explained to the players and drilled on. The first is that the center has to be taught that the backside center linebacker is to be his "backside" block. The frontside guard has to understand that the first man to his outside gap is really considered "on" him because his slant charge places him on his nose at the snap. He is to pass him and block the next outside defender who is playing on the end's nose. The end then must block the "linebacker outside" not "over." The backside tackle is left with a very difficult block to perform. He must cut off his gap man who is charging hard to the inside. The results are that these linemen (center, frontside guard and end) have to block in a special way or adjust their thinking. We feel that with only two minor adjustments we can improve on this plan tremendously and cut down on special recognition problems at the same time.

The center's rule is "backside-on." His rule is not changed, but he must block "backside." The first down lineman to his backside is the defensive guard who is lined up on the puller's outside shoulder.

Diagram 182: Center's block—4-4

The center places his head across the front of the slant charger to stop penetration. Since the defender's goal is to engage the guard, it must be explained that he is considered "on" the guard even though he is lined up in the guard's outside gap. The defender will not be as far away after the snap as he appears to be on alignment.

The frontside guard's rule, inside-outside, is changed to backside linebacker. This is the only major change needed in the rule.

Diagram 183: 6 trap—frontside guard's rule—backside linebacker

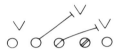

Now both guards are blocking away from the defenders who are trying to cover them. The backside tackle releases down field for the far side half because his man is blocked by the center. This means his rule is changed to lane.

The 6 trap with these two revisions is blocked as follows:

Diagram 184: 6 trap—Notre Dame 4-4

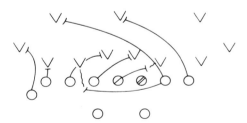

By blocking the frontside guard and center to the backside and having the tackle block the inside linebacker, a strong wall is formed on the inside of the running lane. Stunting by the two center line backers does not upset the play. If they stunt to their outside, the rules pick them up automatically. When the linebackers step into the gaps we block them as a gap set.

Two strong 6 trap plays against the Notre Dame 4-4 are full-back at 6 counter trap and right half at 6 counter trap.

Diagram 185: Fullback at 6 counter trap

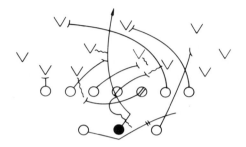

Diagram 186: Right half at 6 counter trap

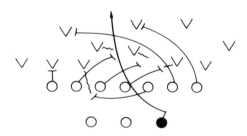

The left end's block may be adjusted according to the play of the linebacker and anchor. If the linebacker is in close and rotating with the flow so that he is in on the tackle, the end can release inside the man on his nose and block the linebacker. Usually a couple of sweep plays to the left will widen the linebacker and take him out of the inside game.

LONG TRAPPING THE NOTRE DAME 4-4

The 3 trap is a very strong play against the Notre Dame 4-4. Only slight adjustments are needed in the rule to clarify the blocking procedure.

Three trap rules

FSE—linebacker inside

FST—inside-linebacker inside
FSG—inside-on
  C—backside-on-over
BSG—Trap in
BST—lane
BSE—lane

One adjustment is that the frontside tackle blocks the "linebacker inside," never "inside." This is a very minor change. We tell him the man to be trapped is the one lining up on his inside shoulder so he automatically blocks the linebacker.

Diagram 187: Frontside tackle block—3 trap versus 4-4

The tackle would have a difficult job blocking the man in his gap with any degree of proficiency because of the hard inside angle charge the defender is using. Even if the tackle could handle the block, the play would take too long to execute if the anchor were trapped instead of the defensive guard. Furthermore, the two-time on the frontside linebacker would be lost.

The only change needed in the rule is that the frontside guard blocks the "backside linebacker" instead of "inside-on." We simply tell him that against the Notre Dame his "inside" block is the "backside linebacker."

The center blocks "backside" as always but he must realize that the first man to his backside is in the guard's outside gap.

Diagram 188: 3 trap versus Notre Dame 4-4

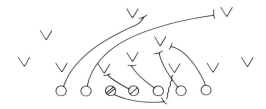

The backside tackle is told to release around the man in his gap because he is blocked by the center.

The strength of the play rests in the fact that four men are sealing the inside of the running lane and the primary defender is two-timed.

The trapper does have a difficult job on the 3 trap, however. First of all, the defensive guard is facing in and charging inside which is ideal for defensive trap reaction. The interior defenders are usually big agile people. The trapper will meet the defender earlier than he usually does. We do not expect the trapper to move the defender. The backs must run for daylight. The hole will open in close to the center with the running lane breaking to the outside.

Diagram 189: 3 trap hole and running lane versus Notre Dame 4-4

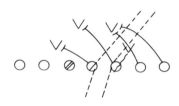

A 3 trap play that hits this lane extremely well is fullback at 3 counter trap.

Diagram 190: Fullback at 3 counter trap

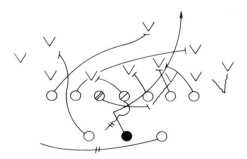

Because we trap so often from the full house "T," many teams will bring their wide defenders in if we don't flex out or slot a back. If this is the case, the frontside end may have to block the outside linebacker on counters against the 4-4.

Diagram 191: Frontside end block—outside linebacker on 3 counter traps

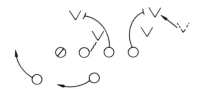

The linebackers will usually flow with the motion so that the tackle can handle the linebacker alone on counter traps.

The left half at 3 trap strikes the running lane at the proper angle and spreads the defense so that pursuit is difficult.

Diagram 192: "Slot," left half at 3 trap versus Notre Dame 4-4

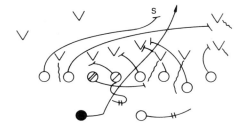

The slotback and end exchange assignments so that the back blocks in and the end screens the linebacker out. The end may also be instructed to seal in on the center area, thereby eliminating the safety.

Diagram 193: Slot formation frontside end

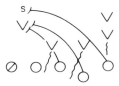

If there is no exchange of assignments between the slot and end, the slot blocks out on the linebacker. There is no longer a two-time on the center linebacker, however.

If the defensive guard is too tough for the trapper, a number of alternatives are possible. First of all, depending on the series, the trap play may be run with a fake at the defensive guard which forces him to commit.

Diagram 194: Slot, left half at 3 trap

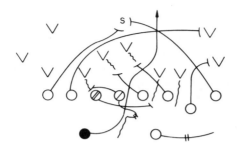

Diagram 195: Left half at 3 trap—FB fake

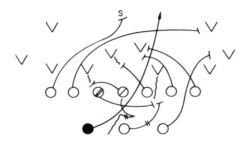

Secondly the defensive guard will not charge hard to the inside if other plays in the series hit to his outside. One example would be to block him in, and slant to his outside or dive to his outside before trapping him out. This may be done with straight ahead blocking and dives or with power blocking. The right half at 3 dive and left half at 2 are good examples of plays to use in conjunction with the 3 trap.

Diagram 196: Right half at 3 dive versus Notre Dame 4-4

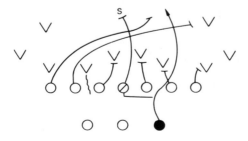

Diagram 197: Left half at 2 versus Notre Dame 4-4

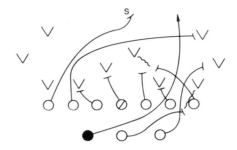

After being driven in a few times, the tackle becomes more outside conscious and may be trapped.

SUMMARY

The short and long trap rules will block the Notre Dame 4-4, but because of the unique alignment, assignments must be reviewed carefully.

Both trap rules should be adjusted slightly to obtain the best results. On the 6 and 3 trap the center blocks the first down lineman to his backside no matter how far over the defender is at alignment. Also on both traps the frontside guards change their regular trap rule to "backside linebacker."

On the 6 trap the backside tackle may now release instead of blocking a lineman.

On the 3 trap the frontside tackle always blocks the linebacker on his side. The backside tackle releases.

On both traps the frontside end's block may be adjusted according to the agressiveness of the defenders.

If the defensive guard's inside charge proves to be a problem for the trapper, the coach can slow the slant charge through the correct choice of plays.

15

TRAPPING THE SLANT LINE DEFENSES

Slanting line defenses are extremely popular in Michigan at the present time and have been for the past few years. The habitually number one class "A" team in the state has used slanting defenses for some time. The University of Michigan recently went to the Rose Bowl by defeating Ohio State and came back the next year with a 9-1 season. Their defense is based on slanting line techniques.

There are many methods that may be employed by slanting defenses. One of the more popular slanting techniques is the one used by the University of Michigan. Their defensive charge starts by taking a jab step with the foot to the side of the slant. In other words, when slanting right, the defender takes a short jab step to the right at a forty-five degree angle with his right foot. With the same motion he drives his left shoulder into the blocker's chest by throwing his left arm down and across the blocker's legs aiming at the far knee. His left foot is driven toward the far side of the blocker. The defender must get under the offensive charge and turn his hips as he drives his shoulder through. On the third step he squares his shoulders and brings his right foot up into the line.

The short jab step with the right foot first gives the defender good base support at contact as he swings his arm and shoulder through.

Diagram 198: Techniques of the slant charge

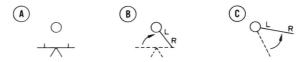

The defender is taught to penetrate only as deep as the blocker's heels. This position is achieved by using two or three short choppy steps after the initial charge.

Diagram 199: Slant charger penetration

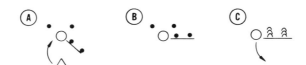

An understanding of the slant technique and the charger's goal is essential when trying to block defenses using slanting charges. Most of these defenses slant their whole line in one direction and cover gaps and void areas with linebackers and secondary rotation.

The slashing charges can be very difficult to block, especially if the linebackers loop or crash in the opposite direction. In preparing to face a slanting defensive team it is usually advised that a team has a variety of blocking methods to cope with the slant.

SMEAR BLOCKING AGAINST SLANTING LINES

One method of blocking slanting lines is to use the smear technique with both sides of the line closing their inside gaps.

Diagram 200: Smear blocking slanting lines

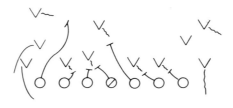

Each man blocks the defender charging into his face. One side will be blocking into the charges while the other is using a cut off or reach block depending on the direction of the slant.

Since smear blocking has been taught as a part of the trap offense, this technique can easily be employed by the total line as one method in defeating the slant defense.

COME AROUND BLOCKING AGAINST THE SLANTING LINE

When the slant line combines slashing linebackers with its defensive maneuvers, more variations than smear blocking are needed if the inside attack is to be effective. Some teams use come around blocking.

Diagram 201: Come around blocking versus the slant line

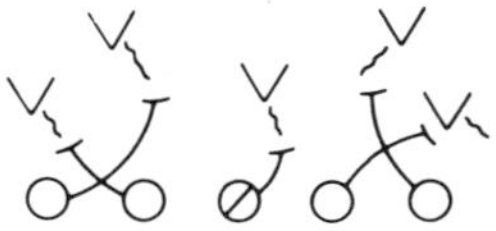

The guards block out against the slant charge from the odd set and the tackles loop around sealing the inside against the slashing linebacker.

This technique is entirely new to most teams because it is used only against looping and slanting teams. This means the line must learn a new technique specifically for a team using slanting stunts. Teaching the tackles to come in around the guards sharply and block up into the linebackers is extremely difficult at the high school level. We prefer to use techniques already in our system to defeat special defenses whenever possible.

ISOLATION BLOCKING AGAINST THE SLANTING LINE

Another successful technique to use against slanting lines is isolation blocking.

Diagram 202: Isolation blocking against the slant line

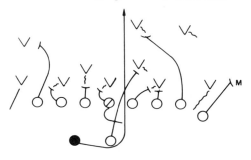

An extra blocker is gained by using a back to pick up the line-backer. This enables the guard and tackle to two-time the slanting linemen. If the slant were in the other direction, the ball carrier would have to cut to the left of the center.

Whenever attacking slanting lines, the backs must run for daylight. The slant causes the holes to move. Sometimes the hole breaks to the backside of the line.

TRAP BLOCKING THE SLANTING LINE

Three of the above techniques, running for daylight, smear blocking, and blocking with a back into the line (isolation) are basic methods used in the trap formula. In addition the trap adds an extra lineman at the point of attack. Because a combination of these successful techniques is possible only through the use of the trap, we feel trap blocking is a powerful weapon against slanting lines.

SIX TRAP VERSUS THE SLANT LINE

The 6 trap formula blocks the slanting line equally well no matter which direction the slant hits.

Diagram 203: 6 trap versus slant left—odd front

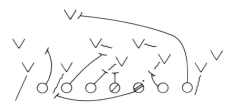

Note: The direction of the slant charge is given from an offensive point of view in this chapter.

The slant left from an odd set presents an almost standard situation. The frontside guard and center two-time the nose man. The guard meets the slant charger head on. The trapper has an easy job because the tackle has stunted to the outside. The backside tackle must block down using the smear technique and tie up the man hitting to his inside. The ends have regular blocks. The hole in this case is extremely wide.

The slant right presents no serious problems. The frontside guard must block his area, however. If the nose guard has charged away, the frontside guard must block across his area in case the line-backer is looping in.

Diagram 204: 6 trap versus slant right—odd front

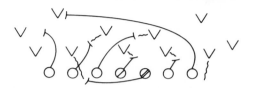

The trapper meets the slanting tackle head on. He will prob-ably be able to do no more than hold the charger to a stand off. The hole will be in close to the center in this case. As can be seen from these two defenses, the hole does move according to the slant.

The frontside tackle has the difficult job. He has to tie up the linebacker as soon as he can. If the linebacker has charged across the hole, he can screen him off to the outside. If the linebacker is drifting into the hole, the tackle must block him with his head in front.

Diagram 205: Frontside tackle blocks on linebacker
6 trap—slant right

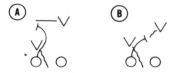

The 6 trap rule blocks the slants from the even line very effec-tively also.

Diagram 206: 6 trap versus slant line left—even front

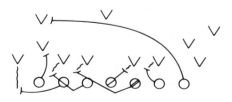

Again, the slant left creates a large hole and good blocking an-gles. The frontside guard blocks outside as does the frontside tackle.

The center meets the backside slant head on. The backside tackle has to tie up the defender charging to his inside.

If the defense slants right, the hole moves to the right.

Diagram 207: 6 trap versus slant right—even front

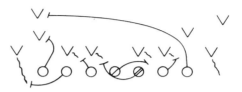

The trapper must get up and into the line in a hurry so as to cut off the inside slant of the guard. The center just rides his guard on out of the hole. The frontside guard and tackle pop up and into their defenders quickly with their head on the inside. Short choppy steps should be used.

SIX TRAP PLAYS VERSUS THE SLANT LINE

If the direction of the slant can be pre-determined by field position or a particular offensive set, the use of certain trap plays can be devastating to the defense. When the odd front is caught slanting left, a play that may go all the way is left half at 6 trap.

Diagram 208: Left half at 6 trap versus slant left—odd front

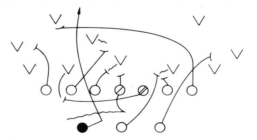

Riding the fullback into the backside aids the tackle with his block and draws the linebackers away from the hole. There is a two-time on the inside of the play while the defender is charging out of the hole on the other side. The back hits the hole straight on and looks for the down field block of the right end.

Naturally, it cannot always be determined which way the defense will charge. Regardless of the direction of the slant, the fullback at 6 counter trap is a good play to use against the even front.

Diagram 209: Fullback at 6 counter trap versus slant left—even front

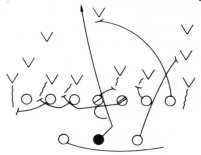

When a slanting line's initial charge is in the opposite direction of the play movement, they attempt to square up quickly. The counter, then, often has the effect of slowing their penetration and charge.

If the defense has a tendency to slant toward the wing man, the counter traps from the wing side work very well.

Diagram 210: Slot—right half at 6 counter trap—slant right—even front

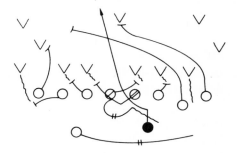

Diagram 211: Slot—wingback at 6 counter trap—slant right—even front

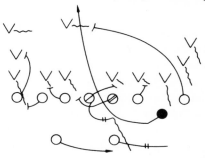

The slant angle assists the countering back in this case because the hole moves to the runner's right. He can square up on his cut and be in a one-on-one situation with the safety right now.

The extra second that it takes the defense to square up its charge and find the ball makes the wing reverse a good play also.

In this case the wing does not have to travel as far to get to the hole. The quarterback should move down the line in a hurry so that the runner can cut with the ball as soon as he sees the opening.

THREE TRAP VERSUS THE SLANT LINE

The 3 trap rule blocks the slanting line very efficiently.

Diagram 212: 3 trap versus slant left—odd front

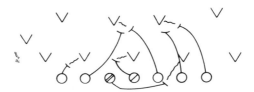

The center blocks the nose man by placing his head in the belt buckle driving him away from the hole using the charger's momentum. His head slides to the hole side when he realizes he is blocking him alone.

The frontside guard blocks to his inside. If the nose man charges away, he turns up field on the first man to show in his face. This is a minor adjustment but it must be worked on to insure success of the play. The frontside tackle and end block the inside linebacker.

The backside tackle and end drop step to the inside and pick up the first man they can reach. They use a smear technique when blocking any man on the line of scrimmage. Against this defense, the tackle may assist on the linebacker.

The trapping guard must pull up into the line and block out on the defensive tackle. The hole in this case will be in close to the center.

The 3 trap is even more effective against the slant right from an odd front. The trapper is blocking a man who is looking to protect an outside seam so his trap block is usually successful.

Diagram 213: 3 trap versus slant right—odd front

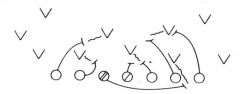

The difficult defender to block is the nose man who is charging into the hole, but he is two-timed by the center and guard. The frontside linebacker is two-timed by the frontside end and tackle. If he is looping to cover against the slant charge, he will be easy prey for them. The backside tackle uses the smear technique to cut off the defender angling to the inside.

The slant to the right from an even front is also a weak defense against the 3 trap.

Diagram 214: 3 trap versus slant right defense—even front

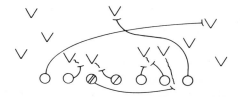

The hole is quite secure because of the two-time on the inside and the outside charge by the defender that is trapped. The backside tackle and end seal inside using the smear technique on the slant chargers. The center blocks against the slant with his head across the front. The frontside end blocks across the hole and up field.

The 3 trap would not be as effective against an even front slanting to the offense's left.

Diagram 215: 3 trap—slant left—even front

The drop step and smear technique must be used by the back-side end and tackle if they are to contain the defender's charge. The center blocks backside, too. The frontside guard and tackle block down on the defensive guard. The trapper has a very difficult job in that the defensive tackle is charging inside and is in good trap reaction position.

Quite often this play will break over the center or way outside if the defender over reacts and gets sealed inside.

Diagram 216: 3 trap versus slant left

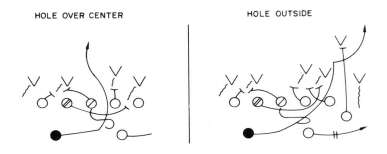

HOLE OVER CENTER   HOLE OUTSIDE

When the slant charger closes to the inside without crossing the line, the trapper many times must seal him inside by placing his head on the outside of the defender or by jumping on top of him if he buries.

Diagram 217: Sealing the slant charger inside

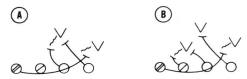

The ball carrier must run under control. If he receives the ball at the proper depth, he will be able to make the adjustments necessary to hit the daylight.

THREE TRAP PLAYS VERSUS THE SLANT LINE

The trap plays will be more effective if the counter traps are run against the slant and the flow traps with the slant. If the defense is slanting toward the wide side of the field most of the time, or every time there is a strong set to the wide side, then the game plan should contain counter traps back into the short side. A good play to use in this situation is fullback at 3 counter trap.

Diagram 218: "T"—fullback at 3 counter trap—slant left—odd front

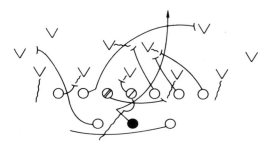

The angle of approach to the hole is directly opposite the slant. This play will be successful in most cases against slanting defenses however, regardless of the direction of the slant because it hits so quickly.

Running the counter with the left half adds backside blocking protection with the fullback. The fake into the center by the fullback also aids in holding the linebackers.

Diagram 219: "T" left half at 3 counter trap
Slant left—odd front

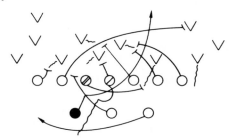

This is not as effective against the even front because the corner linebacker is not blocked.

The same approximate action is simulated with the crossbuck trap except that the right half does not fake around the left end. The fullback still blasts into the line and blocks the first backside defender with the center. Using this fake to the fullback helps to draw the slanting guard back in toward the center, thereby opening the 3 hole a couple of extra feet.

Diagram 220: "T" left half at 3 crossbuck trap versus slant right—even front

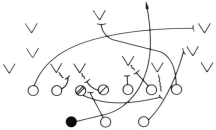

The advantage of this play over the counter against the even front is that the right half blocks the frontside linebacker and the left half heads for the hole at the snap without using a counter step.

Of course the plays often break better if the slants can be predetermined as has been demonstrated, but this is not a necessity. The left half at 3 trap is a good example of a play that works well regardless of the direction of the slant.

Diagram 221: Left half at 3 trap versus slant right—even defense

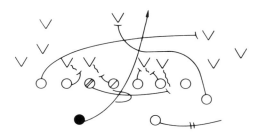

The ball carrier has the option of running for daylight. Against the even defense he may break inside the two-time or outside.

This play is even more successful against the slant to the blocker's left.

The backside tackle and end have a good shot at the men on their inside because they are charging out toward them. The two-time will drive the frontside guard way inside so that the trap block has only to screen off the frontside tackle.

Diagram 222: Left half at 3 trap versus slant left—even defense

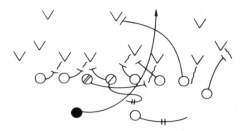

OTHER PLAYS TO USE AGAINST SLANTING DEFENSES

The correct combination of plays used in conjunction with the trap will aid the attack tremendously. Because slant defenses are often taught to penetrate no deeper than the heels of the blocker on their initial charge, we often concentrate our attack on short passes early in the game. This can be particularly effective from the sprint-out pattern.

Diagram 223: Sprintout at 1 versus slant left, even front

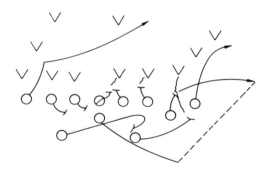

The sprintout will influence the defensive line to charge a little deeper. As soon as the defense starts to penetrate, we trap them.

We also like to pitch around the slant. Often a very effective play is the "quicky" to the short side of the field if the defense is rotating and slanting to the strong side.

The dive hits so quickly that it is difficult for the defensive lineman to recover from his charge before the runner has passed the line of scrimmage.

Diagram 224: Left half at 9 quicky—slant right—odd front

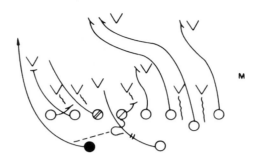

Diagram 225: Right half at 3 dive versus slant left—odd front

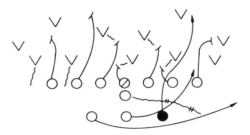

The blocker has only to screen block the defender to open the hole. The runner must cut opposite the slant charge. The guards' objective is to come in contact with the linebackers and run with them.

Plays using isolation blocking can be very effective against the slant also. The left half at 4 is a good example of this.

Diagram 226: Left half at 4 isolate versus slant left

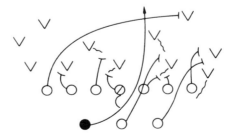

SUMMARY

Trapping Slanting Defenses

A few basic techniques that are traditionally used against slanting defenses are smear blocking by the whole line, come around blocking and isolation blocking. The trap rule makes use of both smear and isolation blocking plus it places an extra lineman at the point of attack. The angles that result are similar to those of the come-around blocks but the trap play enables a team to pull with their quickest linemen eliminating the necessity to teach the tackles to pull around guards. It is very important that the ball carriers run for daylight, not a specific hole, when facing slanting lines.

The 6 and 3 trap rules block slanting odd or even defenses quite efficiently regardless of the direction of the slant. If the direction of the slant can be predetermined by field position or offensive set, a better play selection is possible. For instance, the counter trap can create wide holes when the line is slanting toward the power of the set.

The major adjustment made for this defense is that on either the short or long trap the frontside guard must be taught to turn upfield and block if the defensive nose guard has slanted away from the play.

Faking the fullback into the line on counter and crossbuck traps adds another backside blocker to help seal the gaps.

The plays that are run in combination with the trap against slanting defenses are very important.

16

HOW TO RUN TRAP PLAYS IN A SERIES

Regardless of the formation or series used by a team, the plays must be designed with a variety of blocking methods in order to attack the multiple defenses used today. Many teams use the cross block, trap block, isolation block, and double-team in addition to straight ahead one-on-one blocking and the passing game.

Whatever blocking methods the teams employ, they should make use of all of their techniques in each series of plays when designing their offense. The term series as used here means a group of plays that are designed to look alike.

"T" FORMATION OFFENSE

Fullhouse "T" teams usually plan their attack to place maximum pressure on the defensive tackle area. To do this, they must use the long trap in conjunction with other techniques in each series.

Fullhouse "T" Series from the Tight Line

The basic "T" play run from the fullhouse is the off tackle power play.

Diagram 227: Left half at 2 power

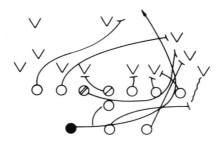

This is a strong power play because there are two defenders hit by two blockers at the point of attack. All running backs are blocking if not carrying the ball, and all blockers have angles on the defenders. The tackle is driven in.

Once this play has established the basic pattern for the series, many options and blocking principles are added. The next logical play to use is left half at 3 trap because the tackle has been driven in by the power blocking until he has become outside conscious. Now he is trapped out.

Diagram 228: Left half at 3 trap

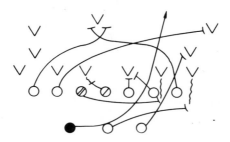

The blocking on this play is identical to the power play except the tackle is trapped out instead of being double teamed in. The backs also run the same pattern.

If the defensive guards veer out to help the tackles, the next play to run in the series is fullback at 4. On this play the line blocks straight ahead while the fullback breaks for daylight off the offensive guard. He will usually cut back slightly against the flow.

Diagram 229: Fullback at 4

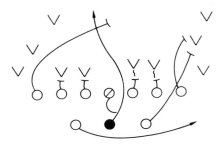

The backs are again running the same pattern.

If the defensive guards close down to stop the fullback from running up the center, the backside guard may be trapped with the 6 trap.

Diagram 230: Fullback at 6 counter trap

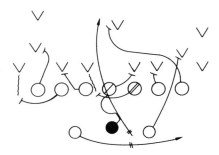

All three backs are moving toward the off-tackle power hole, but the fullback cuts up and slides against the flow.

As soon as the defense starts to key the fullback movement believing he is either the lead blocker or ball carrier, many new options are available to the offense. First, a simple cross buck play with cross blocking is possible. The cross buck fakes the fullback in one direction while handing the ball off in another. An example of this is left half at 2 cross.

This play requires the same quarterback pivoting action as has been used except that he reverses out, away from his first fake, not away from the hole. No new techniques need to be learned by the line to cross block.

Diagram 231: Left half at 2 cross

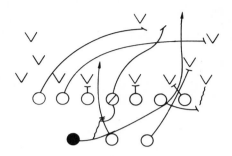

A short trap that coordinates well with any cross buck action is right half at 6 counter trap.

Diagram 232: Right half at 6 counter trap

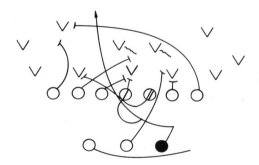

If the defense is keying the fullback or flowing with the basic backfield pattern, this is a very effective counter especially against odd defenses.

Some defenses cross key their center linebackers on any counter motion so well that they jam all plays using counter steps.

An unusual counter trap that takes off all these keys is left half at 6 counter trap with a fullback dive fake.

This is a very delicate play. It should not be used more than a couple of times a game against odd defenses only and against known defensive patterns. To execute this play the quarterback turns toward the 6 hole using an 180° pivot and meets the fullback in the backfield as deeply as possible. He rides the fullback one hitch step

Diagram 233: Left half at 6 counter trap

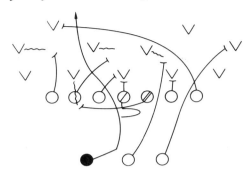

toward the line, drops his right foot back toward the 6 hole and hands the ball to the left half. When the quarterback turns toward the 6 hole, he shows the ball to the defensive tackle. This helps to draw him across the line of scrimmage to be trapped. The left half will find the timing to be about right if he uses a cross over step starting with his left foot moving to his right. He plants his right foot on the second step and cuts up over the guard. The running lane usually breaks back to his left.

The cross over step is used here to get the left half over behind the center away from the trap block and closer to the two-time block. It also keeps the half deep in the backfield before the hand-off in case the trapper misses his block.

The passing game from the tight "T" is rather limited. The most successful passing from this formation is usually done off play action fakes. If the off tackle power is the basic play, the passing game should use the same backfield pattern. Left half at 2 pass is a good example of this.

Diagram 234: Left half at 2 pass

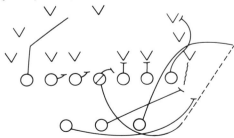

Some teams use a draw fake on most of their passes while other teams fake the pass to run the draw. A team with a poor passer will probably run more draws and use the draw fake to hold down the rush. A common draw run from a full house "T" is the fullback at 6 draw trap.

Diagram 235: Fullback at 6 draw trap

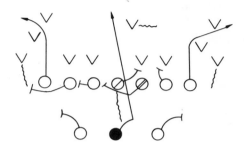

The full house "T" can complement any offense with a series of powerful plays. The power of the "T" lies in its double team blocking and trapping game.

Full house "T" Belly Series—Split line

The belly series from the full house "T" adds to any offense the ability to hit quickly over a wide expanse. Even though the belly series uses mostly straight ahead blocking, the trap adds the ingredients needed in the series to slow the flow of pursuit.

The dive is the basic play around which revolves most of the fakes of the belly series. The backs run the same lanes for each play in the series.

Diagram 236: Right half at 3 dive

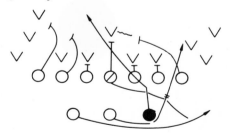

The dive back cuts inside against the flow as soon as he clears the line of scrimmage because the pursuit is following the quarterback movement down the line. All handoffs take place close to the line of scrimmage because the quarterback opens up to the play, stepping to his right and moves down the line, not back off the line. After the handoff he fakes to the fullback and the trail back.

The second basic play in the belly series is the fullback off tackle.

Diagram 237: Fullback at 2

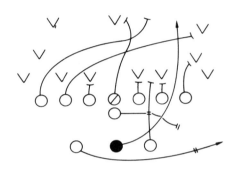

The fullback steps to his right with his right foot first. On his third step he plants his right foot and drives up over the 2 hole area with his left elbow up. The quarterback stays up on the line for the dive fake and then reaches back to hand the ball to the fullback. He then continues on past the fullback faking a pitch to the trailback.

The third basic play in this series is the quarterback keep or pitch option. After faking to the dive man and fullback, the quarterback continues on down the line holding the ball high checking to his inside. If he sees daylight, he tucks the ball and runs. If the defense is on him, he pitches the ball back. The better the fake to the fullback the more open the quarterback will be when he turns upfield.

This is a very limited series as such. All the movement is with the quarterback. The defense will soon key the first step of the fullback and quarterback and shoot linebackers in that direction from an odd set such as the 5-4.

Adding flow traps and counter traps to this series will force the defense to use measures other than the standard split "T" defenses.

Diagram 238: Quarterback option keep or pitch

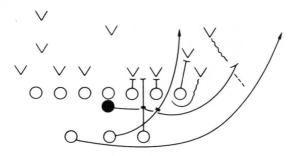

The best trap to use in conjunction with this series for slowing defensive pursuit is the fullback at 6 counter trap.

Diagram 239: Fullback at 6 counter trap

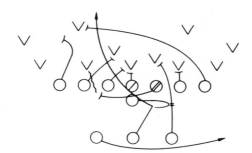

The quarterback opens up to the right half by stepping with his right foot first. He follows through with his left foot, plants it and turns back toward the fullback using a jab step with his right foot to reach the handoff point. The fake to the right half does not have to be a good one. The quarterback's movement to the right and the showing of the ball to the defense will be sufficient action to draw the linebackers with the movement.

The fullback steps to the right with his right foot first, plants it and cuts up toward the center. As he receives the ball, he slides left to the 6 hole following the pulling guard.

Another trap that hits quickly against the flow from this series is right half at 6 dive trap.

The right half should cheat a little wider to give the quarterback time to get back off the line of scrimmage. The quarterback

Diagram 240: Right half at 6 dive trap

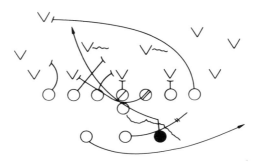

opens up to the right half and starts back to meet him. The right half takes a full step with his right foot and cuts for the 6 hole following the pulling guard. After the handoff, the quarterback continues his fakes to the fullback and trailback. If the counter flow traps are too slow or are being blitzed, flow traps that hit in behind the pursuit will aid the offense. Left half at 3 trap—fullback fake is a flow trap that fits well into the belly series.

Diagram 241: Left half at 3 trap—fullback fake

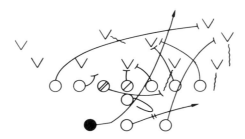

The right half slides to his outside on the dive fake. The fullback angles toward the 2 hole stepping with his right foot first but staying deeper than normal. The left half steps with his right foot first. On his third step he plants his right foot and cuts up into the 3 hole. The quarterback opens up to the fullback, fakes a short ride to him using a hitch step, then turns to the left half by dropping his right foot back and pivoting.

The split "T" belly series is a good series of plays for a high school offense, but any team using this series must incorporate some trap plays to keep the defense honest. The counter traps are usually very effective against split "T" defenses.

PRO SET OFFENSE

The flexible design of pro set offenses enables them to strike over a wide area with sweeps, power plays, traps and quick hitters and at the same time have the threat of a short and long passing game. The off tackle power is a basic play in this series.

Diagram 242: Left half at 2 power—pro set

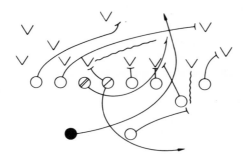

Many teams option block on the end so that if he boxes, the lead back blocks out on him and the ball carrier cuts up, but if he closes, the lead back seals him in and the ball carrier goes wide. The quarterback reverse pivots, hands off and sprints to a deep outside spot.

The left half at 3 trap is run in the series with this power play. When the tackle becomes outside conscious or is fighting the two time hard, he should be trapped.

Diagram 243: Left half at 3 trap—power fake

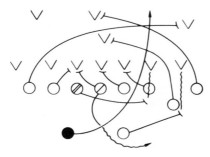

The blocking on this play is identical to that of the power play except the defender is trapped out. The runner will cut up more quickly than on the power. To make this trap look like the power the half passes in front of the quarterback receiving the ball on his second step. When the end is split, the slot man exchanges blocking assignments with him so he hits the inside linebacker in this situation.

This is one play that should not be run the opposite way. To run a 6 trap with the right half, the hand off must be on the inside. If the right half were to come over the top of the quarterback, he would never make the cut.

If a counter trap is desired off this fake, the right half at 6 counter is used.

Diagram 244: Right half at 6 counter trap—power fake

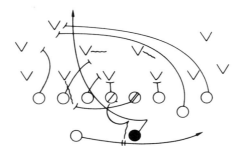

Diagram 245: Left half at 3 Counter trap—power fake

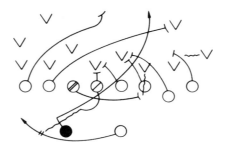

The quarterback reverses out and makes his fake to the left half. He then turns back inside and gives the handoff to the right half. The left half must cheat up if the quarterback is to have time to make a very sincere fake. The right half starts to his right leading with his right foot first, then counters back.

To counter to the right the left half at 3 trap is used.

Another basic play in this series is the quick pitch. This play gets outside right now and therefore spreads the defense considerably.

Diagram 246: Right half at 1 quicky

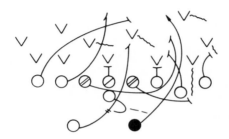

The first defensive reaction is to rotate up and outside to stop the sweep. Again, most teams employ option blocking on the corner so that wide defenders are blocked out and the runner cuts for daylight as soon as possible.

The backside half cuts up over the 3 hole faking the trap after the pitch. This action will help to hold the backside pursuit to a minimum.

The sister play to the quicky pitch is a flow-trap with the left half carrying the ball to the 3 hole.

Diagram 247: Left half at 3 trap—quicky fake

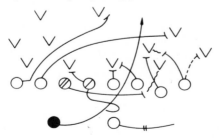

The frontside linebackers start keying the outside movement so they are easily blocked to the outside. The frontside end can be used as an option blocker from his split position. He would automatically block out on the wide linebacker if he just exchanges blocks with the slot man. However, he may be instructed to block inside on a tough linebacker or to turn up field and get the safety depending on the defensive personnel.

The same play going to the left is called right half at 6 trap, quicky fake.

Diagram 248: Right half at 6 trap—quicky fake

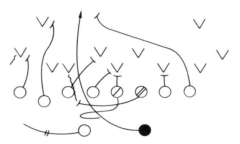

The frontside wide linebacker will be hit by two blockers on this play if no adjustments are made.

If the linebacker takes the outside fake, the slot back should continue on down field and hit the half.

If the defense is pursuing well and it is difficult to break loose with the flow trap, a counter flow trap may be particularly effective from this formation. The wing reverse is an especially good play for this situation.

Diagram 249: Slotback at 6 counter trap—quicky fake

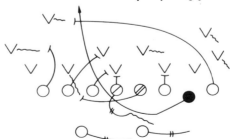

If the trap blocker is having no trouble with the defensive tackle, another trap that may be used against odd fronts is the left half at 6 trap. This play is very effective against teams that are keying the backs real well.

Diagram 250: Left half at 6 trap—quicky fake

When running this trap it is necessary to experiment on timing, but the quarterback can see the left half as he turns out to make his quicky fake so he is able to adjust his steps according to the speed of the halfback. The quarterback should not travel toward the fake on this play. The major part of the fake comes from his head and shoulder movement.

Most teams using this formation pass a great deal. The threat of three immediate receivers puts a real burden on the defensive secondary. If they are pass conscious, the draw trap becomes a major weapon in the game plan. If a defense is dropping back into a zone, the draw will get the runner into the secondary very easily in a pass situation. If the defense is red-dogging in pass situations, the draw may go all the way.

Diagram 251: Left half at 3 draw trap

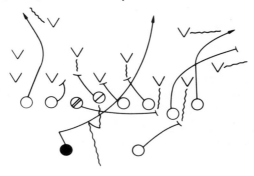

A third basic play used by many teams from the pro set formation is the power sweep.

Diagram 252: Left half at 1 sweep

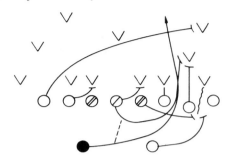

The power sweep blocking enables the offense to double team the end and linebacker and sometimes the tackle at the point of attack. It is the slowest hitting play in the series but a powerful one.

The flow trap off this action would be the left half at 3 trap.

Diagram 253: Left half at 3 trap—sweep fake

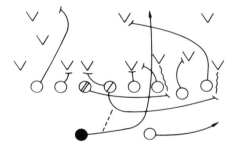

Most defenses will follow the quarterback in this series. After the pitch, he continues down the line and blocks the end. The left half makes a sharp cut up behind the quarterback into the 3 hole.

One of the most effective traps off the sweep action is the back-to-back reverse trap.

The quarterback pitches the ball to the left half and turns up into the line to block. The left half hands the ball off on his inside with his left hand to the slotback who receives the ball with his left elbow up. The exchange should take place behind the right guard so that the slotback has time to square up in the hole. The play may be run with all backs starting at the snap, however the timing can be

Diagram 254: Slotback at 6 reverse trap—back-to-back handoff

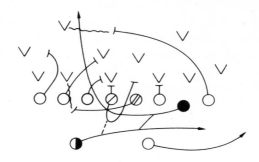

worked out using a man in motion.

Many teams that use the power sweep, pass off the roll-out. On a roll-out pass the quarterback reverse pivots, rolls back and over setting up behind the tackle on the right side.

Diagram 255: Roll-out pass right

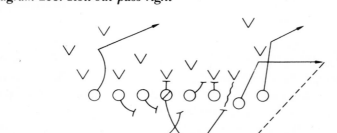

An effective draw play off the roll-out action is left half at 3 draw trap.

Diagram 256: Left half at 3 draw trap—roll-out

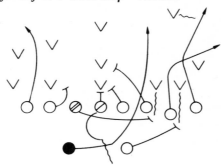

The quarterback carries the ball chest high on his roll out. As he passes the left half who loops back and over, he hands the ball off to him. The exchange should take place behind the right guard.

If a team has a better than average quarterback, their passing is usually done off the sprintout action. The short passing game from the pro set with sprintout action is very difficult to defend against.

Diagram 257: Sprintout at 1 pass

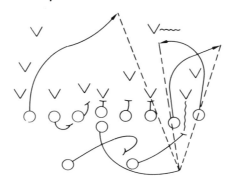

The quarterback sprints on a shallow line to a spot outside of his tackle and four yards deep. From this position he can throw sharply into the flats or down the right side or run. The frontside half blocks on the end while the backside half checks the line then turns back to pick up the backside rush.

As soon as the defense starts to rotate to the side of the play, they are susceptible to the draw trap. The right half at 6 draw trap is a deceptive draw off sprintout action.

Diagram 258: Right half at 6 draw trap—sprintout

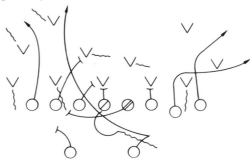

Both halves show a pass block as the quarterback sprints toward the right half. The half holds his pass block for two counts and goes.

"I" FORMATION SERIES

The "I" plays are very similar to the power "T" and pro set plays but the method of attack is different. From each set in the "I" a team usually runs regular sweep plays, off tackle powers, center dives, cross blocks, traps and isolation blocking plus passes. However this attack is built around the tailback position. The basis of the "I" offense is the power play which is the core of each series. The favorite power play for most "I" teams is tailback at 2 power.

Diagram 259: Tailback at 2 power

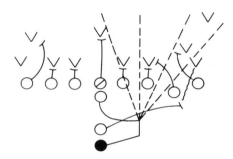

The quarterback reverses out and hands the ball to the tailback three yards deep in the backfield. The tailback moves to his right and squares his shoulders to the line of scrimmage while behind the tackle and then runs for daylight. He may run anywhere from the end to the center in an effort to break into the open.

There are a number of traps possible off this backfield pattern. The tailback at 3 trap looks exactly like the power play.

Diagram 260: Tailback at 3 trap

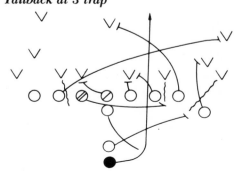

The tailback starts for the corner and cuts up over the tackle. His movement toward the end helps to draw the tackle out for an easy trap block.

The tailback can counter off this movement on the 6 trap.

Diagram 261: Tailback at 6 counter trap

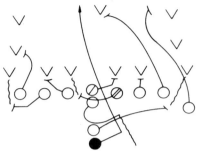

The tailback breaks back to the left at the handoff following the pulling guard.

The fullback at 6 counter trap is a quicker hitting play than the tailback at 6 counter trap. It is also more difficult to key because the defense is concentrating on the tailback.

Diagram 262: Fullback at 6 counter trap

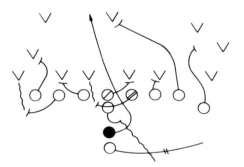

The same play starting to the left side of the line but cutting back would be fullback at 3 counter trap.

The tailback may also run the counter trap back to the 3 hole from the same play action.

The wing reverse is a good trap to use with this series, too. The wing man starts with the snap by stepping to the left with his left foot first. He continues at a slight angle away from the line for two full steps then slants toward the line taking an inside handoff from the quarterback.

Diagram 263: Tailback at 3 counter trap

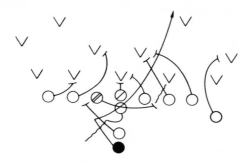

Diagram 264: Wingback at 6 reverse trap

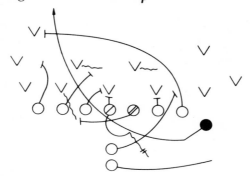

If the "I" is run with one halfback set in his regular position rather than out on the wing, a few more plays are possible in the series. After running the power to the right, a counter trap with the right half is possible.

Diagram 265: "I" right, right half at 6 counter trap

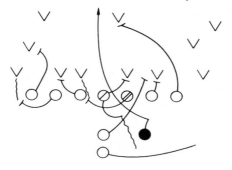

After the defense has been spread out with the pitch, the flow trap to the backside half is a play that will slow the interior pursuit. *Diagram 266: "I" right, right half at 6 trap*

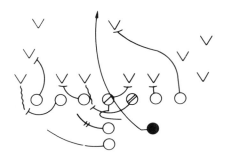

The sprintout pass is a very effective play from the "I." The wing back gives the offense three immediate receivers. *Diagram 267: Sprintout at 1 pass*

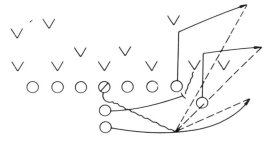

The tailback can be used as a swing-back receiver. *Diagram 268: Tailback at 3 draw trap*

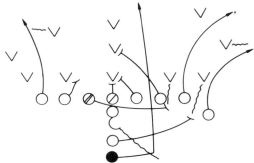

The quarterback reverse pivots and sprints on his normal path to the outside holding the ball at chest height. The fullback blocks out on the end as on the sprintout. The tailback runs a wide deep route then cuts up inside the defensive tackle as he receives the ball from the quarterback.

SUMMARY

Running Trap Plays in a Series

The effectiveness of any offensive series is greatly enhanced by the addition of several trap plays. Flow traps should be run with each series using the same basic backfield pattern as is used for the power plays in the series. A counter trap should be included in the game plan, too.

Whether the passing game is from the dropback or sprintout pattern, a team should have draw traps in their repertory.

One method of employing traps is to drive the tackles in for a number of plays then trap them out. Another is to sweep to spread the defense then trap them up the center. A third is to pass until the defensive line charges hard, then trap them.

IV

Drilling for Proper Techniques in the Running Trap Game

The practice is kept interesting throughout the season by making contests out of certain drills and varying the amount of contact allowed. We keep our drills short and simple. The groups change about every ten minutes or less.

In teaching any fundamentals we follow a general method of teaching progression. Each step gets more difficult or adds new dimensions to the task. In teaching blocking we use the following guide lines:

I. Block dummies
   Head on
   Down field
   Trap blocking
II. Block standing players—allowed two steps
   Head on
   Skeleton groups

   III. Live Tag—all out blocking—defenders can maneuver—
      two hand touch
      Head on
      Down field
      Trap
      Skeleton groups
   IV. Live units—live blockers and tacklers in small units
      Half lines or control groups
    V. Live scrimmage

Even though a technique has been taught, we still go back through this progression as a review and reteaching method every few days on various segments of the offense.

17

DRILLS TO IMPROVE THE TRAPPING GAME

The following drills are a part of our practice plan. They may be used to teach many general techniques for any offense, but they must be used by a team that relies on the trap as a basic part of their attack. The drills are listed according to the type of block the players are to work on. Each of the techniques described in the following drills are an integral part of the trap offense.

DRILLS FOR ONE-ON-ONE BLOCKING

I. Chutes and boards

Chute drills teach the blockers to stay low and keep their feet apart at the same time.

A. The blocker drives a dummy down the board.

B. The blocker attempts to drive a live defender out of the chute.

Diagram 269: Drill—One-on-one blocking—chutes and boards

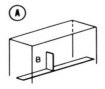 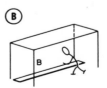

II. Sled drills.

A. Hit down, hit down, hit down

Blockers hit sled from a low stance, recoil to a stance and
hit it on signal again and again.

B. Pass protection. Hit, recoil, pop

From a stance the blocker hits the sled, recoils to a pass
protection stance then pops the sled again.

C. Hit and lift—3 counts

Blockers hit the sled and lift it for three counts.

D. Belly slammer and roll down the line

Blockers fire out low hitting the sled but slamming on to
their bellies. They then flop over to the next dummy
and so on down the line.

E. Hit-Spin-Hit down the line

The blockers hit the sled staying on their feet and spin out
to the next dummy.

LINEBACKER BLOCKING DRILLS

I. Board drills.

The boards teach the blockers to keep a wide base even
though they are in a running position.

A. Run down a board.

B. Block hand dummy off board.

Diagram 270: Drill—Blocking linebackers on boards

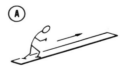 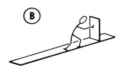

C. Chutes are added to keep the blocker in a crouched
position.

D. The blocker releases through the chute and drives a
man with a hand dummy off the board.

Diagram 271: Drill—Blocking linebackers through chutes

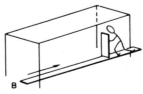

II. Meat grinder

In this live drill the blockers learn to keep a wide base and stay off their knees when hitting linebackers.

A. Arm shields should be used by the linebacker.

B. No blocker is allowed to raise his heels to trip the defender.

Diagram 272: Drill—Meat grinder blocking

III. Sled Drills

These sled drills teach body control from a running position.

A. Two man sled blocking

1. Block the two man sled by starting from a yard back.

2. Block the sled starting from a yard back then spin out to block a moving dummy.

Diagram 273: Drill—Two man sled blocked as linebacker

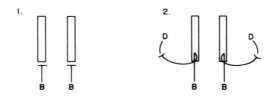

B. Seven man sled blocking

1. The blockers line up at one end of the sled.

2. They block down the line from two yards back by spinning off the sled to the next pad.

Diagram 274: Drill—Spin down the line drill

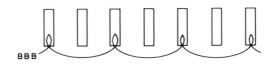

DOWN FIELD BLOCKING DRILLS

I. Release and go

The blockers learn to keep low on their release as well as block down field with this drill.

A. The blockers release under the defensive players' hands.

B. After sprinting four yards they block a player with a hand dummy.

C. Each group of three rotates as a unit after the block.

Diagram 275: Drill—Down field releases

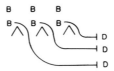

II. Pass receive or block

In this drill the ends learn to block while on their patterns when another end receives the ball.

A. The ends run a pattern.

B. The quarterback throws short passes.

C. Defenders carry hand shields.

D. As one end receives the pass, the other one blocks.

Diagram 276: Drill—Pass receive or block

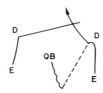

POST AND POWER BLOCKING DRILLS

I. Two-on-one hand dummy blocking

Each lineman learns where to place his head on the post and power situation and how to close the seam.

A. The blockers post and power one defender who protects himself by using two arm shields.

B. One group goes then the other.

Diagram 277: Drill—Post and power, two-on-one

II. Two-on-two—live

The blockers learn to react to live defensive movement.

A. Two defenders line up on two blockers.

B. No shields are used.

SMEAR BLOCKING DRILLS

I. Two-on-two—hand dummy blocking

The blockers learn to cut off a defender in their gap by placing their head across the front of the charger.

A. The defenders shoot low from a four point stance using hand shields on their inside arm.

B. Each blocker fights to get his head and far side arm across the front of the defender.

Diagram 278: Drill—Two-on-two smear blocking

II. Extra points and field goals

The linemen learn to smear block and maintain contact

by swinging their body around in front of the defender
using a wide base for balance.

A. The whole line smear blocks on the snap of the ball.

B. The defenders charge low and hard into all gaps.

C. Shields may be used if no hard contact is desired.

Diagram 279: Drill—Smear blocking on extra points

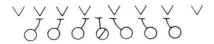

PROGRESSION DRILLS FOR THE TRAPPER

I. Trapper agility

This drill is the first step in teaching footwork.

A. Pulling

1. The coach stands between the pullers.

2. The players walk through their footwork then run
through it.

3. The pullers stay low and pump their arms.

Diagram 280: Drill—Trapper agility

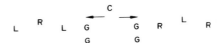

B. Blocking

Dummies are added to teach the pop.

II. Trapper on the boards

The board teaches the trapper to keep a good base when
he pulls.

A. They pull straddling a 12 inch board.

B. They hit a standing dummy with a pop block and lift
and drive the dummy holder off the board.

Diagram 281: Drill—Trapper on the boards

III. Pulling in Chutes

This drill teaches the puller to stay low and get more speed.

    A. Chutes—pulling

        1. They pull through the chutes.

        2. They pull through the chutes straddling a board.

    B. Chutes and dummies

        1. They pull through the chutes, down a board and hit a dummy.

        2. They drive the dummy off the board.

Diagram 282: Drill—Pulling in the chutes

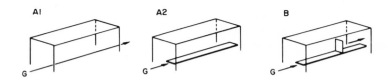

IV. Pulling into the line

This drill teaches the puller to concentrate on staying up in the line as he pulls.

    A. Pull inside boards.

Diagram 283: Drill—Pull into the line

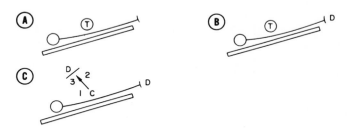

        1. Place a board behind the puller and a tire beside him.

        2. The puller must not step back onto the board.

    B. Pull inside board and hit dummy

        1. A dummy is added to the drill.

        2. The dummy may be pushed down or held up.

    C. A live center is added for foot work.

        1. Place a dummy over the guard for the center to block.

        2. The center must learn to block with both shoulders equally fast.

V. Brush elbow

This drill also teaches the puller to stay up and into the line as he pulls.

    A. Place a center, guard and tackle on the line with the puller.

    B. Put dummies over the puller and the frontside guard.

    C. The man who is being trapped carries a hand shield.

    D. The puller is to brush his inside elbow on the butts of the interior line as he pulls.

Diagram 284: Drill—Brush elbow

VI. Steal the flag

This drill not only makes the puller turn in, but it teaches him to stay low and dip for the pop block also.

    A. Place the guard—center—guard on the line.

    B. Put dummy holders over them. Change the sets.

    C. Place a cloth on the ground inside the hole being trapped.

    D. The puller steps down the line, dips and grabs the cloth, and blocks a man moving with an air dummy.

Diagram 285: Drill—Steal the flag

VII. Trapper multiple reaction

This drill teaches the trapper to react to any action by the defender. He learns to scan the area visually as he comes down the line.

A. Puller only
1. Place the puller and center on the line.
2. Lay a long dummy in the hole and place two players kneeling with hand dummies at the hole area.
3. The coach tells a player to stand up just after the snap.
4. The puller is to react and hit the standing defender.
5. If no defender stands, the puller must cover the dummy on the inside simulating a defender buried on the inside of the running lane.

Diagram 286: Drill—Trapper multiple reaction

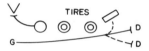

B. Trapper multiple reaction—interior line
1. The same drill is used except all offensive players tackle to tackle are involved.
2. Players with hand dummies are added for defense.
3. The coach changes the defensive sets each time the drill is run.

Diagram 287: Drill—Live multiple reaction

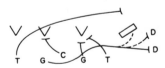

VIII. Blaster drills for trapper
Pulling into the blaster increases the pullers' strength and agility.

A. Pull for strength
1. Pullers line up at blaster facing at a slight angle.
2. They pull down a board and hit into the blaster from various distances.

Diagram 288: Drill—Blaster pulling

B. Pull and react
   1. They repeat the above action.
   2. Standing dummies are added so that they must recover from the blaster and hit.

Diagram 289: Drill—Blaster pulling and dummy blocking

IX. Changing defenses
   The total line is involved in reacting to changing defenses. This is a control group situation run during the drill period.
   A. The whole line runs their trap plays.
   B. The defensive sets are played by men with hand dummies.
   They move on the snap.
   C. The defense changes their set after the line is down.

Diagram 290: Drill—Changing defenses

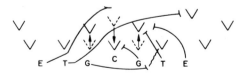

X. Live tag scrimmage
   The total offensive reaction to various defenses is tested by running the trap plays at a live defense. The runners

are only tagged, however.

A. Offensive and defensive units line up.

B. No tackling is allowed.

C. The defenses shift sets.

D. Trap plays are run.

Diagram 291: Drill—Live tag

18

CORRECTING COMMON
FAULTS IN THE TRAP

The drills discussed in the last chapter will correct most of the general faults inherent in the trap play. However, the coach must be able to recognize why a problem is occurring and know the best method for solving it. Many times it appears that a player is missing a block, but in fact he is hitting a defender well. He may, however, be misinterpreting the rule and blocking the wrong man. Sometimes a player just can't handle his assignment and can't figure out why. The coach must know exactly what to tell the player. He has to know what adjustments can be made.

The following discussions cover a number of common faults that a coach will face when using trap plays. A few solutions to the problems are suggested.

LINE PLAY

Puller's stance

The first fault that is common to most every trapping team is the leaning puller. The coach must detect this early in the season so as not to let a bad habit get started. The puller should have the same stance on all plays. If he displays a low butt or turned out toe when he is to pull, his stance will give the trap away.

In teaching men to pull, we stress that the worst thing a player can do is to lean the way he is going to pull. This puts all his wieght on the foot he has to move first. His weight will have to shift back before he can move. This is time lost, not gained.

Drilling in the chutes and down boards in races in prepractice should correct any lean.

Center's steps

The next problem for the puller is getting by the center. The center must fire out down the line by stepping with the foot to the side he is blocking. The guard's first step should be on the spot where the center's foot was before the snap. We tell the guard to step on the center if he is in the way. We also tell the center what will happen if he lags with his first step.

If the guard's head is hitting the center as the center comes down the line, the guard's first step is wrong and/or the center is too slow. To correct this problem we go back to progression drills number "4 c." It is best to always use air dummies in drills and have the defender's charge. It is not realistic to hit big standing dummies. The defense must move in if the drill is to be of any real value.

Diagram 292: Center steps and blocks

Don't let the guard raise up to get over the center. If he gets too high, pulling drills run in the chutes will help to keep him down.

Head placement on blocks

A major fault in a trapping offense is letting the defense penetrate too far into the backfield. All blockers must put their heads in front to stop the penetration of any defender divorced from him half a man or more. The blocker must anticipate the charge, however. Teach him to go for where the defender will be not for where he is.

Diagram 293: Aiming the block

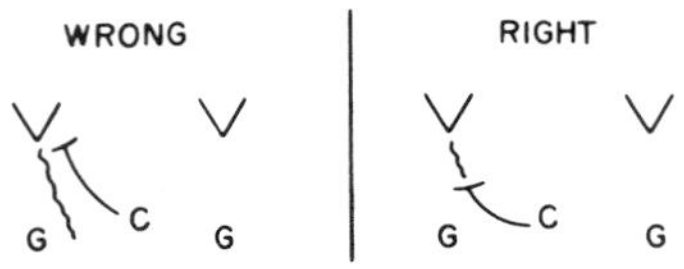

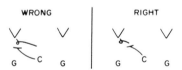

Usually the center will be the worst violator of this technique. He has an easy job when the defense is in an odd set and not red-dogging, but when he faces an even set he must get down the line and cover for the puller. To assist the center in doing this, we place a small, fast man in a low stance over the puller in drills. The center works until he can fire down and get his head in front. The defender has an air dummy on his inside arm. This drill works!

If the defender is playing soft and rolling back and out of the blocker's hit when he puts his head in front, the blocker must adjust and aim his helmet into the rib cage. Stress keeping the elbows high on all blocks.

Diagram 294: Head placement versus non-charging defender

Diagram 295: Head placement on the post and power block

The height of the head placement is very important on the post and power block. The post man should be low and power man high. If the post man is in the power's way, the post is probably so high the defender is handling him physically and throwing him in the second blocker's way.

Drill live on the post and power block if the post is too high. Make the defender get on all fours and charge out low. This will force the post man to hit lower.

The trapper must put his head on the inside of the defender he is trapping. A common fault is that he pulls so deep that he can't get back into the line in time to get his head inside a good defender that is closing down. We correct this fault with the "brush elbow drill" or "steal the cloth drill." We never let the trapper get away with careless head placement in practice or a game even if knocks the defender flat. We also cut film loops of this fault and make the pullers view them before every game.

Fire Out

Many times a player will start thinking it is easier to block a charging defender that is down the line if he doesn't fire out. He believes he can stand up and wait for the charge and then step in front of the defender.

This cautious play will sometimes work on a quick but weak defender. Soon, however, a defender will knock the non-charging blocker back into the puller's path and destroy the trap. Do not allow any frontside blocker, especially the guard, to stand up and play the defensive charge. No matter how many misses a blocker has, he must fire out in practice until he can block the defender to his inside.

Diagram 296: Frontside charge

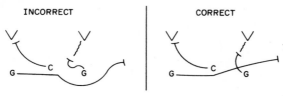

This fault can be corrected by bringing it to the frontside blocker's attention and putting some hard chargers over them in the "brush elbow drill." Again, we like to run film loops of this mistake early in the season.

Rule Interpretation

High school players get mixed up easily on their rules. First of all, they must be drilled enough to recite the correct rule for the play. Early in the year the center will forget many times and cover for the wrong guard. To avoid such simple errors the players should use a word call system at the line of scrimmage whereby they can double check their blocks with their team mates.

Using a word call system as was described in the chapters on "the trap rules in action" will help greatly to eliminate misinterpretations of the defensive set. A tackle may read the defense as calling for a post and power block, but the guard reads the situation as a smear technique. Drill on trap plays in unit work at least two days a week, plus running traps in scrimmage will help the players with this problem. During the group drill sessions, the defenses are changed on each play and the blockers are made to recite their rules and point out their blocks until the coach is sure each player is interpreting the rule correctly. This type of instruction is easy to do while running the group drill No. IX "Changing defenses."

BACKFIELD PLAY
Diagram 297: Speeding up the counter step

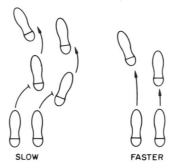

SLOW   FASTER

Footwork

The backfield must also undergo close observation when correcting faults in a trap play. If the hole is closing before the backs get to the opening on counter traps, the back's steps and alignment should be studied. Usually they are too slow on their first delay step. This can be speeded up by having the back step more directly at the hole.

Alignment

The alignment may be varied to speed up the play also. If the back is set closer to the line, the play will break sooner. If the back stands too erect on his delay step, he is not only slower, but he will give the counter play away. Whenever a back stands up and throws an arm in the air, the defense knows he is countering. Keep the backs low on their first step on the counter traps.

Diagram 298: Variation of alignment

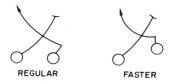

REGULAR   FASTER

Running Form

The trap hole is always shifting. When the defense is changed, the running lane is changed. If a back is constantly missing his running lane on the trap, the coach should first check his running form. Backs that run too low and hit with their heads down find it difficult to adjust to the shifting and drifting nature of the running lane on traps. We drill on running for daylight which means the backs must keep their weight under control.

Running Lanes

Many backs get hung by arm tackles around the neck on a trap play because they run too close to the trapper. To eliminate the uncertainty of the trap block we teach the backs to run close to the two-time or angle block on the inside of the hole.

Last year our best runner had a great deal of difficulty in finding the open field after he cleared the line of scrimmage. He

Diagram 299: Running the trap hole

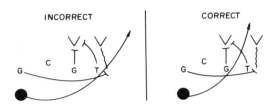

would follow the trapper and break through the hole, but he would then continue on the same path rather than turn up field toward the goal posts. This is a common error in running traps.

Diagram 300: Angle of approach to hole—no cut

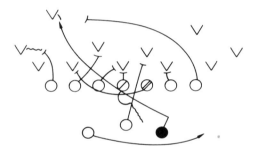

As the runner clears the line of scrimmage he must square his shoulders to the goal line and read the secondary. If he squares up, he can see his backside releasers and cut off their blocks if possible.

Diagram 301: Squaring up in the hole

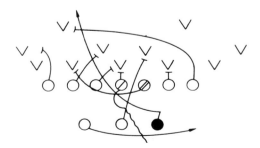

CHECK SHEET: CORRECTING FAULTS
IN THE TRAPPING GAME

Line Play

Defense recognizes a trap call before the snap

1. Puller's stance changed
2. Leaning puller

Slow puller

1. Incorrect stance
2. Leaning in pulling direction
3. Looping too deep
4. Too high on pull

Looping puller

1. Incorrect footwork
2. Center's steps too slow
3. Frontside guard not firing out

Defensive penetration along the line

1. Linemen not blocking with head in front of defender
2. Linemen not anticipating spot of contact
3. Linemen blocking across the line of scrimmage, not down it

Defense breaks the two-time block

1. Post man too high
2. Power man not closing the seam
3. Improper head placement

Linemen block the wrong defender

1. Quarterback call out "trap" distinctly in huddle
2. Linemen recite trap rule over and over
3. Double check blocks using a word call system at the line of scrimmage
4. Review terminology definitions in the rule

Backfield Play

Incorrect timing-reaching the hole early

1. Adjust alignment

2. Adjust running lane

Incorrect timing-reaching the hole late

1. Do not use counter step
2. Adjust alignment
3. Runner too erect

Runner misses the hole

1. Running with head down
2. Running with too much forward lean
3. Adjust running lane

Runner caught by arm tackles in line

1. Run next to two-time block
2. Lower shoulders
3. Widen running base

Runner can't evade secondary tacklers

1. Square shoulders to the goal line in secondary
2. Cut behind backside releasers
3. Review running lane
4. Releasers too deep

SUMMARY

As with all other facets of the game, the coach must be alert to the weak points of his trap plays. Once the coach identifies the flaws, he should then institute a series of steps that will correct the problems. The first step is to point out to the player what he is doing incorrectly. This may be done through demonstration, film, chalk talks, etc. The second step is to review the correct techniques and rules to be used in execution of the play. The third step is to provide the correct drill and proper amount of practice time needed to enable the player or group of players to perform adequately.

Some of the key points to observe in line play on the trap are the puller's stance, the center's steps, head placement on blocks so as to stop penetration, the post blocker's charge and rule application. The backfield's crucial areas are adjusting their footwork and alignment for timing, and turning up into the running lanes so as to keep their shoulders square to the goal line.

Index

scheme vs. 5-2
crashing L.B.